Toys & Accessories

Handyman Club Library™

Handyman Club of America
Minnetonka, Minnesota

Toys & Accessories

Printed in 2010.

CREDITS

Tom Carpenter
Creative Director

Mark Johanson
Book Products Development Manager

Chris Marshall
Editor, Series Coordinator

Dan Cary
Photo Production Coordinator

Steve Anderson
Assistant Editor, Senior Book Production Assistant

John English
Project Designer, Contributing Writer

Marti Naughton
Series Design, Art Direction & Production

Kim Bailey
Photographer

Mark Macemon
Contributing Photographer

Eric Sorensen, Jon Hegge
Project Builders

Bruce Kieffer
Technical Illustrations

Brad Classon
Production Assistance

ISBN 10: 1-58159-084-9
ISBN 13: 978-1-58159-084-5
7 8 / 15 14 13 12 11 10
© 1999 Handyman Club of America

Handyman Club of America
12301 Whitewater Drive
Minnetonka, Minnesota 55343
www.handymanclub.com

Contents

Cedar Bird Feeder (64)

Double-drawer Chessboard (72)

Domino Set (50)

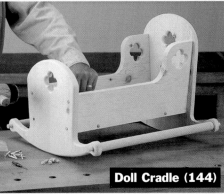

Doll Cradle (144)

Mantel Clock (8)

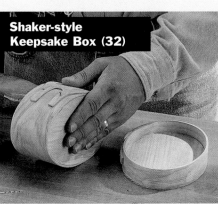

Shaker-style Keepsake Box (32)

Knife Storage Block (44)

Up-and-Away Wind Chime (102)

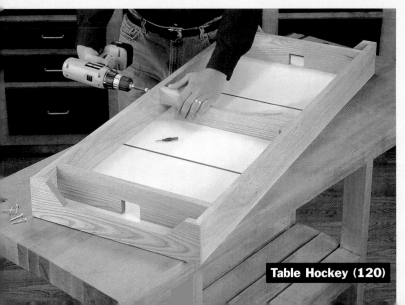

Table Hockey (120)

Bentwood Reader's Bin (80)

Tambour Breadbox (150)

Inlaid Tea Tray (16)

Ball-&-Cup Game (114)

Mini Treasure Chest (24)

Collapsible Band Saw Basket (58)

Dial-A-Bird (132)

Crosscut Trivets (92)

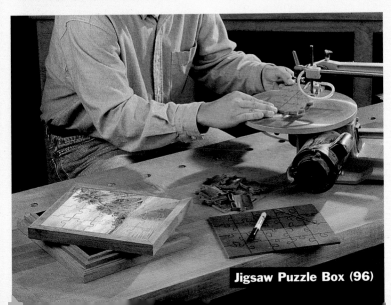
Jigsaw Puzzle Box (96)

Bathtime Boat (86)

Introduction

Whether you build the projects in this book for your own amusement or give them away to family and friends, the gratification of working with wood will be all yours. As you page through the 23 projects in this new volume, *Toys & Accessories,* published exclusively for Members of the Handyman Club of America, you'll find a broad assortment of both toys and keepsakes to suit a variety of tastes and woodworking skill levels. If a challenge is what you're after, we've provided some specialized techniques to try, like applying veneer, steam-bending, and cutting round tenons. Have you ever built a tambour door or used your drill press like a lathe? Here's your chance. There are plenty of simpler projects here as well, if you'd like to spend some time in the shop building with a youngster you know.

Each project is presented with complete cutting and shopping lists, detailed drawings, beautiful color photographs of the project as it's being built and straightforward step-by-step instructions. Time to buy some lumber and get started!

BUYING HARDWOOD FROM A LUMBERYARD

Nearly every project in this book is built from hardwood. Your local home center probably stocks a few species of hardwoods, like oak, maple and cherry. These boards generally are planed to ¾ in. thick, jointed flat on the edges and cut to standard widths and lengths. Within the lumber industry, lumber of this sort is categorized as "S4S", which stands for Surfaced Four Sides. All of this surface preparation at the mill translates to higher prices for you, but it may make the most sense to buy S4S lumber if you don't own a thickness planer or jointer to prepare board surfaces yourself.

To find specialty or thicker hardwoods, you'll need to shop at a traditional lumberyard. A good lumberyard will offer a wide selection of hardwoods in random widths and in an assortment of thicknesses and grades. In addition to S4S, you'll find S2S lumber (planed smooth on two faces but the edges are rough), and roughsawn boards that are simply cut from the log, dried and shipped to the lumberyard. Roughsawn boards are the least expensive option, but you'll need to do all the surface prep yourself.

Unlike your home center, lumberyards use a quartering system for identifying board thickness. For instance, a 1-in.-thick roughsawn board will be labeled as 4/4 (four ¼-in. units), a 5/4 board will be 1¼ in. thick, and an 8/4 board will be 2 in. thick. Also, you'll buy stock by the *board foot*. A board foot equals one running (lineal) foot of a board that's 12 in. wide and 1 in. thick. To calculate precisely how many board feet of material you'll need for your project, multiply the length by the width by the thickness (expressed in inches) then divide that number by 144.

Before you start a project, find out what dimensions your local supplier has in the species you need, and draw cutting diagrams for your project parts, so you can estimate more accurately. Also, be aware that even lumber that's been planed on both sides at the mill will likely require additional planing, so buy wood that's at least ¼ in. thicker than you need.

S4S

S2S

Roughsawn

Options for reducing lumber thickness

Toys and accessories, more than other woodworking projects, have parts with smaller proportions that require thinner stock. But purchasing hardwood lumber less than ¾ in. thick isn't economical—even if you can find it. And the specialty hardwoods featured in some of the projects in this book are sold in 4/4 or thicker dimensions only. What do you do if the project calls for ¾-, ½- and ¼-in.-thick parts? Inevitably, you'll have to reduce your lumber thickness. Here are your best options.

In cases where ¾-in. stock is what you need, buy 4/4 lumber and run it through a power planer to remove the extra ¼ in. Be sure to plane both faces of the board as you go, making alternating passes and planing with the grain to minimize tearout.

Turn to the band saw for producing workpieces thinner than ¾ in. The technique, called *resawing*, involves passing the board on edge through the saw blade to slice the board in two. Resawing is safe and economizes lumber, but it can be a bit tricky to master. This is because the band saw blade will attempt to follow the wood grain and wander off your cutting line. To minimize wandering, clamp a shop-built resawing jig next to the blade to support the workpiece vertically as you cut. The jig should have a long edge that tapers to a point, and this is the edge that touches the workpiece. As you cut, the jig allows you

OPTION 1: Planing stock to thickness

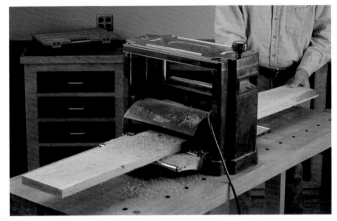

Plane hardwood in ⅟16-in. or shallower passes to keep from overwhelming your planer motor, burning the lumber and prematurely dulling the planer knives. Wear hearing protection, and be prepared to produce a mountain of chips, even when planing off ¼ in. of material or less.

to pivot the workpiece from side to side while feeding it into the blade, to compensate for blade wander.

You can also reduce wandering by tuning up your band saw first, and resaw with a sharp 6-tooth-per-in. hook-tooth blade in as wide a size as will fit your band saw.

Clean up any saw marks left on your workpieces using a sharp hand plane or by running them through a power planer.

OPTION 2: Resawing stock on a band saw

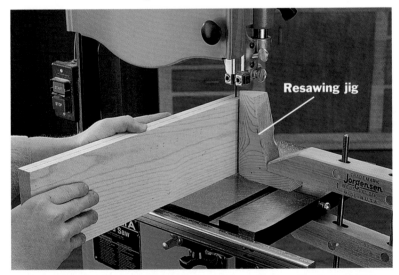

Position a resawing jig perpendicular to the band saw blade so the tapered edge of the jig touches the board. Adjust the position of the jig and board until the blade lines up with your cutting line. Clamp the jig to the saw table. Then start the saw and push the board through the blade, guiding it against the resawing jig as you go. You may need to pivot the workpiece right or left to keep the blade on track.

Resawing will leave blade marks on the workpiece. Remove these marks and smooth the sawn board face by running it through the power planer. If you don't own a planer, a hand plane will also do the trick.

Mantel Clock

The mantel clock is one of the oldest clock types, sized to fit neatly on a hearth. But you don't need a fireplace for an excuse to build this heirloom-quality project. Its compact size will be equally attractive on a bookshelf or side table. Made of cherry, our design features a split-frame glass panel to highlight the brass pendulum and clock face as well as an elegant crown and base that you can make easily with a router.

Vital Statistics: Mantel Clock

TYPE: Clock

OVERALL SIZE: 10½W by 16⅞H by 5¼D

MATERIAL: Cherry, cherry plywood, glass

JOINERY: Rabbets, dowel-reinforced butt joints

CONSTRUCTION DETAILS:

· Crown and base profiles are routed onto the ends and edges of individual parts, which are then laminated together
· Face frame chamfered on the inside and outside edges
· Glass held in place with removable retainer frame
· Hole cut in back panel for easy access to clock movement
· Clockwork kit installed in case

FINISH: Satin tung oil

Building time

 PREPARING STOCK
2-3 hours

 LAYOUT
2-3 hours

 CUTTING PARTS
3-4 hours

 ASSEMBLY
3-4 hours

 FINISHING
2-3 hours

TOTAL: 12-17 hours

Tools you'll use

· Jointer
· Planer
· Table saw
· Router table with 45° piloted chamfer bit, ½-in. roundover bit, ¼-in. cove and bead bit
· Jig saw
· Drill/driver
· Doweling jig
· Clamps

Shopping list

☐ (2) ½ × 6 in. × 8 ft. cherry
☐ (1) ¾ × 6 × 12 in. cherry
☐ (1) ¼ in. × 2 ft. × 2 ft. cherry plywood
☐ (1) ³⁄₃₂ × 6¼ × 13 in. glass
☐ ¼-in. dowel
☐ #6 × ½ in. panhead screws with washers
☐ #4 × ¾ in. brass flathead wood screws
☐ 6 × 6-in. brass clock face, battery-powered quartz movement, brass pendulum
☐ Wood glue
☐ Finishing materials

Mantel Clock

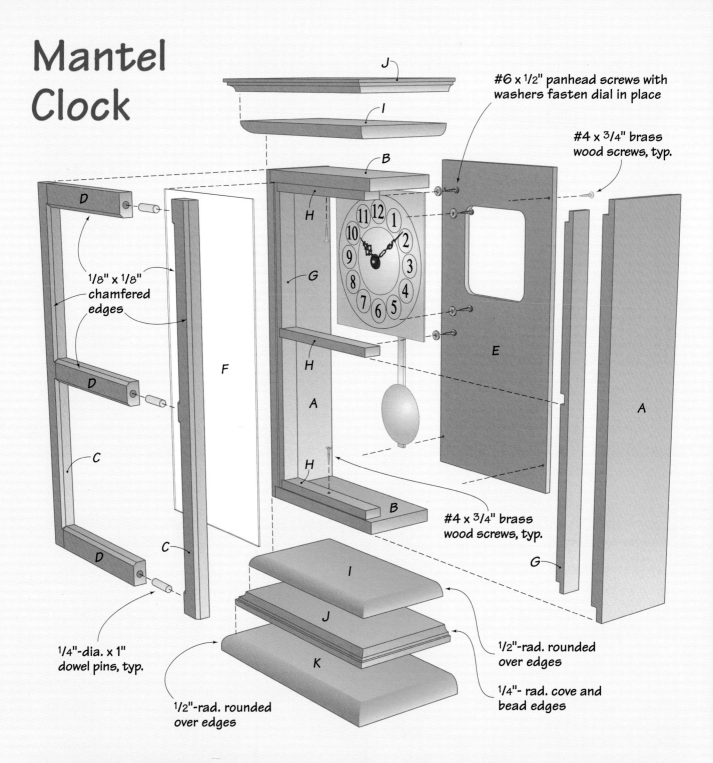

J

I

#6 x 1/2" panhead screws with washers fasten dial in place

#4 x 3/4" brass wood screws, typ.

B

D

H

1/8" x 1/8" chamfered edges

G

H

D

F

A

C

E

H

D

B

C

A

#4 x 3/4" brass wood screws, typ.

G

1/4"-dia. x 1" dowel pins, typ.

I

J

1/2"-rad. rounded over edges

K

1/4"- rad. cove and bead edges

1/2"-rad. rounded over edges

Mantel Clock Cutting List

Part	No.	Size	Material
A. Carcase sides	2	1/2 × 3 1/4 × 14 1/8 in.	Cherry
B. Carcase top, bottom	2	1/2 × 3 × 7 in.	"
C. Frame stiles	2	1/2 × 7/8 × 14 1/8 in.	"
D. Frame rails	2	1/2 × 7/8 × 5 3/4 in.	"
E. Back	1	1/4 × 7 1/4 × 14 1/8 in.	Cherry plywood
F. Glass	1	3/32 × 6 7/16 × 13 1/16 in.	

Part	No.	Size	Material
G. Retainer stiles	2	3/8 × 3/4 × 13 1/8 in.	Cherry
H. Retainer rails	3	3/8 × 3/4 × 6 1/8 in.	"
I. Roundover top, bottom	2	1/2 × 4 1/4 × 8 1/2 in.	"
J. Cove top, bottom	2	1/2 × 4 3/4 × 9 1/2 in.	"
K. Roundover base	1	3/4 × 5 1/4 × 10 1/2 in.	"

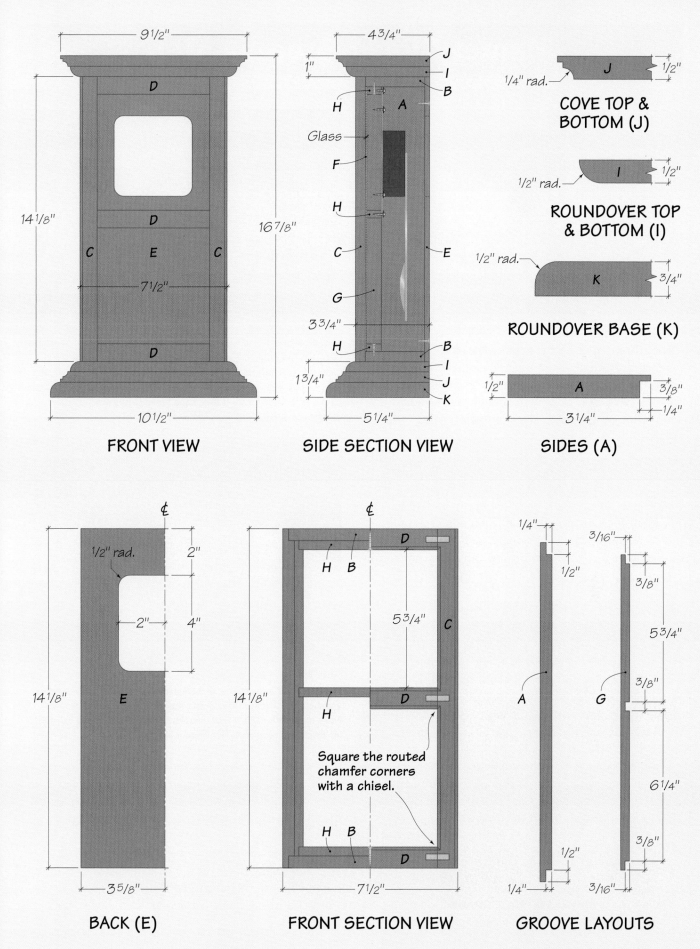

9 1/2"

D

14 1/8"

C   E   C

7 1/2"

D

16 7/8"

D

10 1/2"

FRONT VIEW

4 3/4"

1"

J
I
B

H   A

Glass

F

H

C   E

G

3 3/4"

H

B
I
J
K

1 3/4"

5 1/4"

SIDE SECTION VIEW

1/4" rad.   J   **1/2"**

COVE TOP &
BOTTOM (J)

1/2" rad.   I   **1/2"**

ROUNDOVER TOP
& BOTTOM (I)

1/2" rad.   K   **3/4"**

ROUNDOVER BASE (K)

1/2"   A   **3/8"**
1/4"

3 1/4"

SIDES (A)

1/2" rad.   **2"**

2"   **4"**

14 1/8"

E

3 5/8"

BACK (E)

D

H   B

5 3/4"   C

D

H

Square the routed
chamfer corners
with a chisel.

14 1/8"

H   B

D

7 1/2"

FRONT SECTION VIEW

1/4"

3/16"

1/2"

3/8"

5 3/4"

A   G

3/8"

3/8"

6 1/4"

1/2"

1/4"   **3/16"**   **3/8"**

GROOVE LAYOUTS

MAKE THE CARCASE

❶ Cut the carcase parts: Rip and crosscut the carcase sides, top and bottom to size from ½-in. stock, according to the *Cutting List* dimensions, page 10.

❷ Rout rabbets into the ends of the sides for the carcase top and bottom pieces. Cut these rabbets on the table saw using a dado blade. Set your dado blade to ½ in. wide, and raise it to a height of ¼ in. Cut a ½-in.-wide rabbet into each end of both side pieces.

❸ Cut the back panel rabbets. First, install a sacrificial fence on your saw's rip fence to keep the dado blade from damaging the metal fence. Raise the dado blade so it cuts into the wooden sacrificial fence to a height of ⅜ in. so only ¼ in. of the blade protrudes out from the saw fence. Lay each side piece with the end rabbets facedown on the saw table, and cut a rabbet into one long edge of each (**See Photo A**).

❹ Glue up the carcase: Dry-fit the carcase top and bottom pieces into their rabbets in the sides. Be sure the top and bottom fit fully into their rabbets, or the crown and base assemblies will not fit properly later. Sand the faces of the parts smooth now, while they're still accessible. Spread glue into the rabbets, and clamp up the top, bottom and sides. Adjust the clamps until the carcase is square.

❺ Make the back: Rip and crosscut ¼-in. cherry plywood for the back panel. Then, lay out and cut the center access hole, using the *Back* drawing, page 11, as a guide. Cut out the access hole with a jig saw. Drill a ½-in.-dia. pilot hole at each corner of the cutout area first, to make turning the jig saw easier as you cut.

BUILD THE FACE FRAME

❻ Cut the stiles and rails to size: Rip and crosscut

PHOTO A: Cut rabbets across the ends and along one long edge of each side piece using a dado blade on the table saw. These rabbets form recesses for the carcase top and bottom, as well as the plywood back panel. Attach a sacrificial wood fence to your saw fence to protect the metal fence from the dado blade.

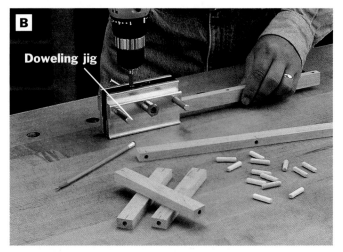

PHOTO B: Drill holes in the face frame rails and sides so you can assemble these parts with dowels. A doweling jig ensures that the holes are positioned precisely across each joint and keeps the drill bit straight in relation to the workpiece.

the two face frame stiles and three rails from ½-in. stock. Lay the face frame parts into position on the clock carcase and be sure that the overall face frame fits flush with the outside edges of the carcase.

❼ Drill the face frame dowel joints: Measure and mark for dowel holes on the rails and stiles. The center rail should be centered on the length of the stiles. Then clamp each face frame part in a doweling jig and drill ½-in.-deep dowel holes, centered across the

PHOTO C: Square off the inside chamfered corners of the face frame with a chisel. Lay out these corners first with a pencil and square, then pare up to your layout lines.

PHOTO D: Rout the roundover and cove and bead profiles into the ends and along one edge of the base and crown parts. Mill the end grain first, then rout the long grain; otherwise the bit could tear out the corners of your finished edges.

thickness of the parts (**See Photo B**). Use a ¼-in.-dia. drill bit for boring these holes, and mark your drill bit with masking tape to keep from accidentally drilling the holes too deeply.

8 Glue up the face frame: Cut six 1-in.-long dowels, and spread an even coating of glue onto each dowel. Insert the dowels into the face frame parts, and clamp the face frame to hold the dowel joints tightly closed until the glue dries.

9 Rout the face frame chamfers: Install a 45° piloted chamfer bit in your router, and adjust the bit depth to ⅛ in. Set the face frame on a non-slip router pad, and rout counterclockwise around the inside edges of the face frame openings. Work carefully, keeping the router base held firmly against the face frame as you go. Use a pencil and combination square to square off the corners where the router bit couldn't reach, and pare chamfers into the face frame corners with a sharp chisel to square them off (**See Photo C**). Then, cut long chamfers along the outside edges of the face frame with the router at the same bit setting as you used for the inside chamfers. Be careful not to chamfer the ends of the face frame; they should butt flush against the crown and base.

ASSEMBLE THE CROWN & BASE

To avoid milling tiny molding and attaching it to the clock, or using wide manufactured crown molding instead, we simply routed profiles into larger blanks of cherry stock for the crown and base, then laminated these parts together. The crown is composed of

two parts—one with a roundover profile and one with a cove and bead profile. The base is made of three pieces: two roundovers sandwiching a layer with a cove and bead profile.

10 Make the roundover parts: Rip and crosscut the roundover top, bottom and base to size. Note that the base is made of ¾-in. stock, while the other roundover parts are ½ in. thick. Set up a piloted ½-in. roundover bit in the router table, and rout the profiles in two passes of increasing depth, to minimize burn marks

PHOTO E: Glue up the crown and base first, then glue these completed assemblies to the clock carcase. Glue alone will bond these parts sufficiently, so no additional fasteners are needed.

PHOTO F: Cut rabbets and dadoes into the retainer stiles for the retainer rails. Make these cuts on the table saw with a dado blade, and hold the parts against the miter gauge. We installed an auxiliary fence on the miter gauge to keep the dado blade from tearing out the grain on the retainer stiles.

PHOTO G: Install the glass and retainer frame with a pair of brass wood screws—one through the retainer top rail and one through the bottom rail. Countersink these screws.

left on the workpieces. Rout the ends of these workpieces first, which are more likely to chip when the bit exits the workpiece. You'll clean up these corners when you rout the long edge of each part. Once the routing is complete, sand the parts smooth.

⓫ Make the cove and bead parts: Rip and crosscut the cove and bead top and bottom to size. Use the

same router techniques for milling the profiles that you used in Step 10, routing the ends first, then the edges (**See Photo D**). Sand these parts smooth and to remove all burn marks.

⓬ Glue up the crown and base: Spread glue over the mating surfaces of the crown parts and clamp them together. Be sure the back edges are flush and the cove and bead pieces overhang the roundover piece evenly. Glue and clamp the base parts together similarly with the bottom cove and bead piece sandwiched between the roundover bottom and roundover base. For more clarification on the orientation of these parts, see *Side Section View,* page 11.

⓭ Install the crown and base on the carcase: Spread an even layer of wood glue over the top and bottom ends of the carcase, and set the crown and base in position. Use spring clamps to hold the parts together and keep them from shifting while the glue dries (**See Photo E**).

INSTALL THE RETAINER & GLASS
The glass is held in place in the clock case with a stile-and-rail retainer frame and a couple of screws. This way, the glass remains removable, should it ever need replacing.

⓮ Cut the retainer parts: Surface plane ½-in. cherry stock down to ⅜ in. thick for the retainer parts. Rip and crosscut the two glass retainer stiles and three retainer rails to size.

⓯ Mill rabbets and dadoes into the retainer stiles for the rails. Notice in the *Groove Layouts* drawing, page 11, that the retainer stiles are rabbeted on the ends and dadoed across the middle to house the retainer rails. Make these cuts on the table saw with a dado blade set to a width of ⅜ in. and raised ³⁄₁₆ in. above the saw table. Mark the rabbet and dado locations on each of the stiles, and cut the dadoes and rabbets carefully with the stiles held against the miter gauge (**See Photo F**). Sand the retainer parts smooth.

⓰ Assemble the retainer and install the glass: Dry-fit the retainer rails and stiles together, then glue and clamp the parts. Be sure the retainer frame is flat as well as square. Once the glue dries, set the glass in place in the clock case, drill countersunk pilot holes through the top and bottom retainer rails, and fasten the retainer and glass in place with two #4 × ¾-in. brass wood screws (**See Photo G**).

PHOTO H: Attach the quartz clock movement and hands to the clock face, according to the kitmaker's instructions.

PHOTO I: Fasten the brass clock face to the top portion of the retainer frame with six panhead sheet metal screws and washers. Pushpins serve as a handy way to hold the clock face in place as you adjust it, prior to installing screws and washers.

ASSEMBLE & MOUNT THE CLOCKWORK

⑰ Follow the instructions that come with your clock works to install the quartz movement and hands on the brass clock face (**See Photo H**).

⑱ Mount the clock face: Set the clock face into place on the top retainer frame opening inside the clock carcase. Shift the face up and down, right and left until it is positioned evenly within the retainer frame. Hold the brass face in place temporarily with pushpins while you install it with #6 × ½-in. panhead machine screws and washers. Drill pilot holes for these screws to keep them from splitting the retainer parts (**See Photo I**).

FINISHING TOUCHES

⑲ Prepare the clock for finishing: Disassemble the clockwork, and remove the retainer and glass from the clock carcase. Sand any remaining rough edges and surfaces smooth with 220-grit sandpaper.

⑳ Apply the finish. We used wipe-on tung oil to enrich the natural wood tones and grain of the cherry. After each coat, rub down the surfaces of all the wood parts with #0000 steel wool, which "burnishes" the finish and removes any surface irregularities.

㉑ Assemble the clock: Reinstall the glass, retainer and clock face. Fasten the back panel into its rabbets in the carcase back with four #4 × ¾-in. brass flat-head wood screws (**See Photo J**). Drill countersunk pilot holes for the screws.

PHOTO J: Apply your finish of choice to all of the wood clock surfaces, then install the clock back with brass flathead wood screws, driven through the back and into the rabbets in the carcase back.

Inlaid Tea Tray

Impress your guests and cut down on the number of trips you make to the kitchen when you build this generously sized serving tray. The finger-jointed corners are attractive as well as sturdy, and the decorative veneer inlay adds a sophisticated touch.

Vital Statistics: Inlaid Tea Tray

TYPE: Serving tray

OVERALL SIZE: 17W by 3H by 24L

MATERIAL: Cherry, cherry plywood, veneer inlay

JOINERY: Finger, biscuit, dado joints

CONSTRUCTION DETAILS:

· Tray bottom made of two sheets of ¼-in. cherry plywood laminated together and surrounded by a mitered and biscuited cherry frame

· Decorative veneer inlay on tray bottom installed into a shallow rabbet cut around the perimeter of the top plywood panel

· Frame ends attach to sides with finger joints

FINISH: Satin tung oil or polyurethane

Building time

PREPARING STOCK
1 hour

LAYOUT
2-3 hours

CUTTING PARTS
4-5 hours

ASSEMBLY
2-3 hours

FINISHING
1 hour

TOTAL: 10-13 hours

Tools you'll use

· Table saw
· Dado blade
· Power miter saw
· Router table with ½-in. straight bit
· Scroll saw
· Drum sander or drill press and drum sander attachment
· Biscuit jointer
· Clamps

Shopping list

☐ (1) ½ × 8 in. × 6 ft. cherry

☐ (1) ¼ in. × 2 ft. × 2 ft. cherry plywood

☐ #20 biscuits

☐ ¹/32 × ½ in. × 6 lineal ft. decorative veneer inlay strip

☐ Wood glue

☐ Finishing materials

Inlaid
Tea Tray

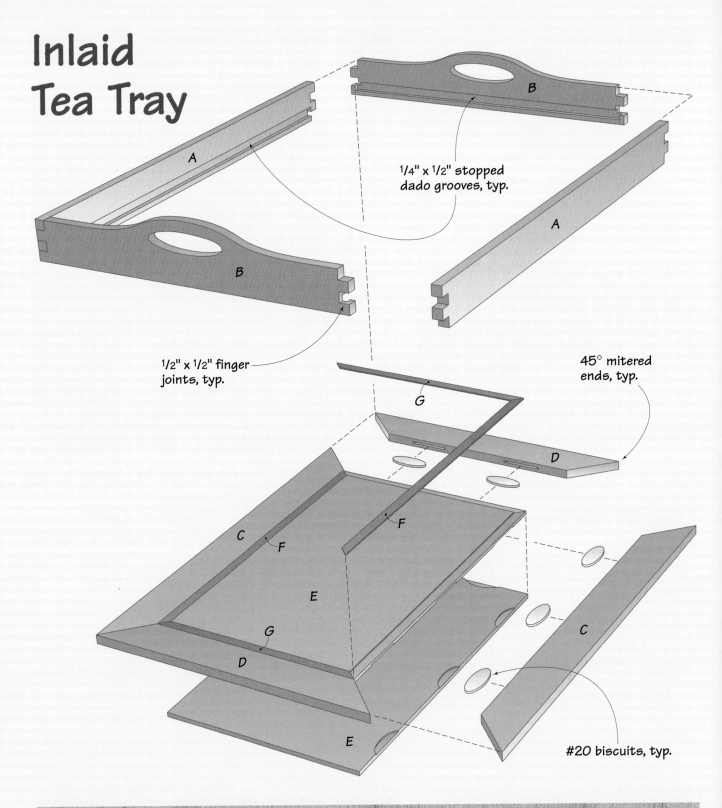

B

A

1/4" x 1/2" stopped
dado grooves, typ.

A

B

1/2" x 1/2" finger
joints, typ.

G

45° mitered
ends, typ.

D

F

C

F

E

G

D

C

E

#20 biscuits, typ.

Inlaid Tea Tray Cutting List

Part	No.	Size	Material	Part	No.	Size	Material
A. Tray sides	2	$1/2 \times 2 \times 24$ in.	Cherry	**E.** Bottom panels	2	$1/4 \times 11^{15}/16 \times 18^{15}/16$ in.	Cherry plywood
B. Tray ends	2	$1/2 \times 3 \times 17$ in.	"				
C. Frame sides	2	$1/2 \times 2^{1}/4 \times 23^{7}/16$ in.	"	**F.** Long inlays	2	$1/32 \times 1/2 \times 20$ in.	Veneer strips
D. Frame ends	2	$1/2 \times 2^{1}/4 \times 16^{7}/16$ in.	"	**G.** Short inlays	2	$1/32 \times 1/2 \times 13$ in.	"

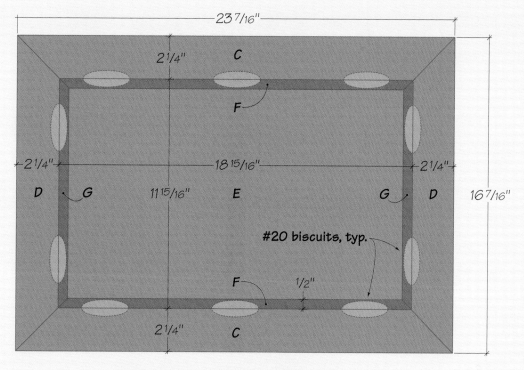

TOP VIEW ASSEMBLED BOTTOM

23 7/16"

2 1/4" C

F

2 1/4" 18 15/16" 2 1/4"

D G 11 15/16" E G D 16 7/16"

#20 biscuits, typ.

F 1/2"

2 1/4" C

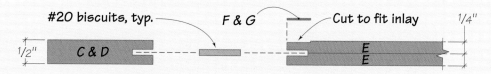

#20 biscuits, typ.

F & G Cut to fit inlay 1/4"

1/2" C & D E E

DETAIL: BOTTOMS, FRAMES & INLAYS

1/2" 1/2" A 2"

1/4" x 1/2" stopped dado grooves, typ. ₵

FRONT VIEW TRAY SIDES

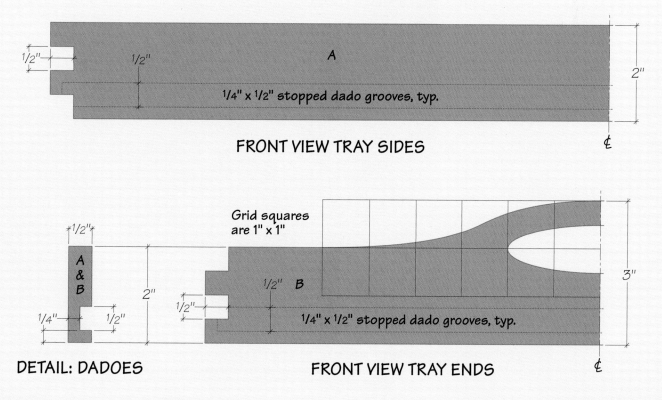

1/2" Grid squares are 1" x 1"

A & B 2" 1/2" B 3"

1/4" 1/2" 1/2" 1/4" x 1/2" stopped dado grooves, typ. ₵

DETAIL: DADOES   **FRONT VIEW TRAY ENDS**

MAKE THE TRAY SIDES & ENDS

1 Rip and crosscut workpieces for the tray sides and ends, according to the dimensions given in the *Cutting List,* page 18.

2 Mark the tray ends for the handles and finger joints. Start by drawing a 1 × 1-in. grid pattern on the tray ends, then transfer the curved handle profile and cutout shown in the *Front View Tray Ends* drawing, page 19, onto the parts. Next, lay out the finger joints. Mark ½ × ½-in. finger joints on the tray ends and sides **(See Photo A)**. Notice on the exploded view drawing (page 19) that the fingers on the tray sides match, and the fingers on the tray ends match. In order to interlock, the fingers start on the top edges of the tray sides and on the bottom edges of the tray ends.

3 Lay out the bottom grooves. The plywood bottom will fit into ½-in.-wide, ¼-in.-deep dadoes cut into both the tray sides and ends. Lay out these dado cuts on the inside faces of the tray parts, ¼ in. up from the bottom edges. The grooves on both sets of parts must stop ¼ in. from the ends of the workpieces, or you'll cut through the closest fingers.

4 Cut the finger joints: Set up a ½-in.-wide dado blade on the table

PHOTO A: Lay out the finger joints on the ends of the tray side and end pieces. Use a combination square to mark the joints. Draw X's on the waste areas.

PHOTO B: Mill the finger joints with a ½-in.-wide dado blade. Attach an auxiliary wood fence to the miter gauge to hold the workpieces securely. Since the fingers match on like workpieces, clamp them in pairs to cut the fingers in both parts at once. NOTE: *Work carefully when setting up these cuts—even slightly misaligned cuts can produce poorly fitting finger joints.*

Fence marks indicate leading and trailing edges of router bit

PHOTO C: Cut the bottom panel grooves in the tray sides and ends on the router table. When cutting these stopped dadoes on the tray sides and ends, mark the leading and trailing edges of the bit on the router fence so you know where to start and stop the cuts.

PHOTO D: Cut the curved handle profiles and cutouts on the scroll saw. You'll need to drill an access hole for the blade first, in order to start the handle cutout.

saw and raise it ½ in. above the saw table. Attach a tall auxiliary fence to the miter gauge to support the workpieces as you cut them on end. Then stack the tray sides together and clamp them to the miter gauge, checking to be sure they are square to the saw table. Cut away the waste between the fingers. Follow the same procedure for cutting the tray end fingers (**See Photo B**).

5 Rout grooves for the bottom panel. Install a ½-in. straight bit in the router table, and align the bit and fence to follow your bottom dado layout lines on the tray sides and ends. Then mark the leading and trailing edges of the router bit on the fence, and use these references to start and stop the dadoes as you cut them in the tray parts (**See Photo C**). Square the ends of these stopped dadoes with a chisel.

6 Cut the handle profiles and cutouts on the tray end pieces with a scroll saw (**See Photo D**).

7 Sand the tray side and end pieces smooth. A drum sander works well for sanding the profiles.

BUILD THE BOTTOM

8 Rip and crosscut the frame side and end pieces to width and length. Cut 45° miters on the ends of these four parts with a miter saw (**See Photo E**).

9 Cut and glue the plywood bottom panels together to create a ½-in.-thick blank. Spread glue on one face of each panel, and laminate them together. Sandwich the glue-up between clamps and long cauls to distribute clamping pressure evenly and produce a tight glue joint (**See Photo F**).

PHOTO E: Rip and crosscut the frame end and side pieces to size, then miter-cut the ends of the parts to 45°.

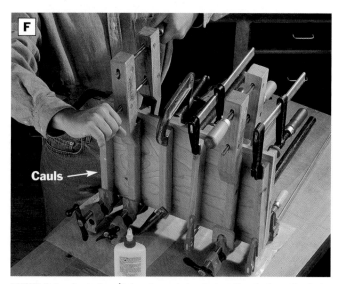

Cauls ➞

PHOTO F: Laminate two ¼-in. plywood sheets together to form the bottom panel. Clamp up the plywood on both sides with long wood cauls to press the sheets tightly together until the glue dries.

PHOTO G: Lay out and cut #20 biscuit slots to join the frame side and end pieces to the bottom panel. Clamp the parts in a bench vise to hold them securely when you cut the slots.

PHOTO H: Rout a shallow rabbet around the top face of the bottom panel for the veneer inlay strips. Install a ½-in. straight bit in your router table to cut this ⅟₃₂-in.-deep rabbet. Practice on scraps first and test the fit of the strips in the rabbet.

PHOTO I: Miter-cut the corners of the decorative inlay strips using the 45° fence on a combination square and a sharp utility knife. Hold the knife as square to the inlay as you can when making the cuts, so the mitered joints will meet flush.

PHOTO J: Install the inlay strips on the bottom panel rabbets. Glue one piece at a time to the plywood, and press it firmly in place with a couple of clamps and a wood caul. Cover the inlay with wax paper before clamping on the caul to keep the parts from sticking together.

10 Lay out and cut #20 biscuit slots to join the frame sides and ends to the bottom panel **(See Photo G)**. Plan for two biscuits on each end piece and three per side piece. Cut all the slots.

11 Rout a ½-in.-wide, 1⁄32-in.-deep rabbet around the top face of the bottom panel for the decorative veneer inlay strips. Use a straight bit in the router table to make these cuts **(See Photo H)**.

12 Cut and fit the bottom panel inlay strips. Instead of cutting these strips all at once, you'll get better results if you work your way around the bottom panel, cutting one piece at a time, then fitting and cutting the adjacent strip. Trim 45° miters on the ends of the inlay strips with a sharp utility knife and a combination square **(See Photo I)**. For best visual effect, try to cut the corner joints so the inlay pattern continues around the corners without abrupt breaks in the pattern. NOTE: *Most decorative inlay strips have a pattern repeat for seaming and cornering.*

13 Glue the inlay strips to the bottom panel: Install the pieces one at a time in the shallow rabbets. Clamp the inlay in place with a wood caul protected by wax paper, in case the glue seeps through the inlay. Allow the glue to dry before removing the caul and moving on to the next strip **(See Photo J)**.

14 Install the frame side and end pieces on the bottom panel: Spread glue on the mating surfaces of the parts and into the biscuit slots. Insert the biscuits and clamp up the assembly **(See Photo K)**. A frame clamp or strap clamp works well for holding the

PHOTO K: Attach the frame sides and ends to the inlaid bottom panel with glue and biscuits. Dry-fit the parts together first with the biscuits in place. Once the pieces are glued and fitted, install a frame clamp around the assembly and tighten.

PHOTO L: Spread glue onto mating surfaces of the finger joints, slip the bottom into its grooves and clamp up the tray. Install clamps both lengthwise and widthwise to hold the finger joints closed in two directions.

mitered corners closed while the glue dries. Then sand the bottom assembly smooth.

ASSEMBLE THE TRAY

15 Dry-fit the tray sides and ends around the bottom panel assembly with the bottom panel inserted in its grooves. Then disassemble the parts, spread glue in the gaps between the fingers, and fit the tray together **(See Photo L)**. Do not glue the bottom panel into its grooves so it can "float" freely. Clamp up the tray both lengthwise and widthwise, and measure diagonally from corner to corner to be sure the tray is square. Adjust the clamps to make corrections.

FINISHING TOUCHES

16 Smooth the entire project with 220-grit paper, easing all the edges lightly as you go. Apply three coats of clear tung oil to the tray. Sand between coats with 320-grit wet/dry paper or #0000 steel wool, and remove the dust with a tack cloth. If your tray will be used to serve beverages, topcoat with three layers of polyurethane varnish instead of tung oil, to protect it from moisture stains.

Pirates, Spanish galleons under sail and secret caves filled with gold doubloons were the inspiration for this mahogany and walnut treasure chest project. It's a perfect place for a child to store secret treasures, yet handsome enough to adorn an adult's dresser as a catch-all for pocket change, keys or jewelry.

Mini Treasure Chest

Vital Statistics: Mini Treasure Chest

TYPE: Jewelry/valet chest

OVERALL SIZE: 5½W by 6¼H by 8L

MATERIAL: Honduras mahogany, walnut

JOINERY: Butt, dado joints

CONSTRUCTION DETAILS:

· Lid arch formed by a seven-piece glue-up that is hand-planed to shape

· Box front and back tapers are hand-planed to shape

· Curved walnut lid strapping is drawn onto flat stock with a compass, then cut to shape on the band saw

· Bottom floats in grooves in the box front, back and ends

· Lid attached to box with brass piano hinge

FINISH: Spray-on satin lacquer

Building time

PREPARING STOCK
2 hours

LAYOUT
1-2 hours

CUTTING PARTS
4-5 hours

ASSEMBLY
2 hours

FINISHING
1 hour

TOTAL: 10-12 hours

Tools you'll use

· Table saw

· Dado blade (optional)

· Router and ¼-in. straight bit (optional)

· Band saw

· Back saw

· Clamps

· Hand plane

· Belt sander

· Drum sander

· Drill/driver

· Chisel

Shopping list

HANDYMAN CLUB OF AMERICA

☐ (1) 4/4 × 8 in. × 6 ft. Honduras mahogany

☐ (1) ½ × 4 in. × 2 ft. walnut

☐ (1) 5/8 × 8-in. brass piano hinge

☐ (1) 1-in. brass hook latch, mounting screws

☐ (2) 1-in.-dia. ring pulls

☐ Wood glue

☐ Spray adhesive

☐ Finishing materials

Mini Treasure Chest

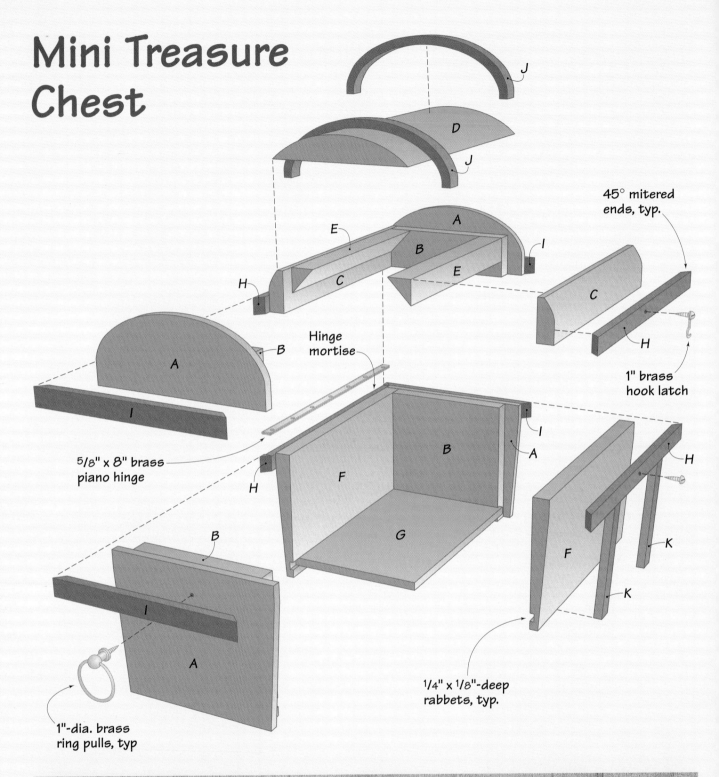

J

D

J

45° mitered
ends, typ.

E

A

B

I

E

H

C

C

H

1" brass
hook latch

A

B

Hinge
mortise

I

A

H

B

H

5/8" x 8" brass
piano hinge

F

I

K

G

F

B

K

I

1/4" x 1/8"-deep
rabbets, typ.

A

1"-dia. brass
ring pulls, typ

Mini Treasure Chest Cutting List

Part	No.	Size	Material	Part	No.	Size	Material
A. Chest ends	2	$1/4 \times 6 \times 5$ in.	Mahogany	**G.** Bottom	1	$1/4 \times 4 1/4 \times 6 3/4$ in.	Mahogany
B. End build-ups	2	$1/2 \times 5 1/4 \times 4$ in.	"	**H.** Trim front, back	4	$1/4 \times 1/2 \times 8 1/2$ in.	Walnut
C. Lid front, back	2	$3/4 \times 1 1/4 \times 7 1/2$ in.	"	**I.** Trim ends	4	$1/4 \times 1/2 \times 5 1/2$ in.	"
D. Lid top	1	$1/4 \times 4 1/2 \times 7 1/2$ in.	"	**J.** Lid strapping	2	$1/2 \times 1 3/4 \times 5 1/2$ in.	"
E. Fillets	2	$3/4 \times 3/4 \times 6 1/2$ in.	"	**K.** Box strapping	4	$1/4 \times 1/2 \times 3 1/2$ in.	"
F. Box front, back	2	$1/2 \times 4 \times 7 1/2$ in.	"				

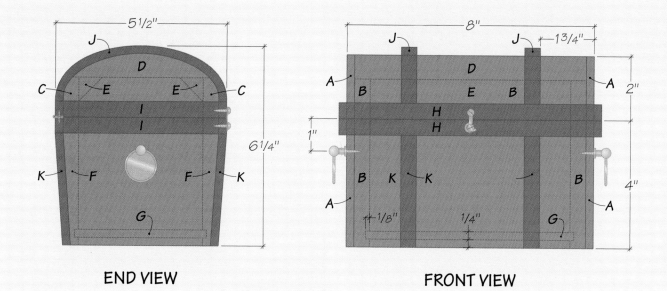

5 1/2"

J

D

C — E   E — C

I
I

6 1/4"

K — F   F — K

G

END VIEW

8"

J   J   1 3/4"

A   D   A   2"

B   E   B

H
H

1"

B   K — K   B   4"

A   A

1/8"   1/4"   G

FRONT VIEW

Align chest
end (A) with
end build-up
(B) here

A   B

Cut along this
line after joining
& shaping
pieces A & B

Grid
squares
are 1" x 1"

1/4"   1/4"

LAYOUT: CHEST ENDS & END BUILD-UPS

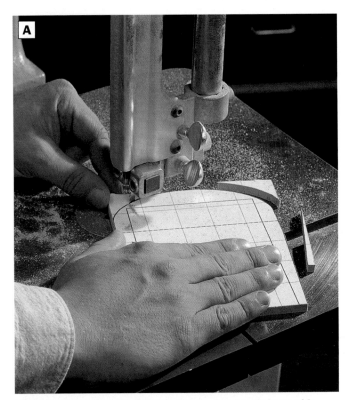

PHOTO A: Stick paper templates to the chest end workpieces with spray adhesive, and cut out the parts on the band saw. Leave the patterns in place temporarily, to mark the end build-up locations.

PREPARE THE MAHOGANY STOCK

This project is made mostly of mahogany in several thicknesses—¾ in., ½ in. and ¼ in. Most lumberyards will not stock mahogany milled to these specific thicknesses, so you'll have to start from a thicker 4/4 (about 1-in.-thick) board. Before you begin the project, take time to evaluate how you will size down your 4/4 mahogany to produce stock with the correct thickness for all of the treasure chest parts. To make most efficient use of your mahogany, resaw the stock on the band saw if you have one, then plane the resulting thinner boards to the thicknesses you need. (*For more on resawing and surface planing, see page 7.*) This way, you'll waste only a fraction of the mahogany as opposed to just planing down the stock.

MAKE THE LID & BOX ENDS

❶ Cut the chest ends to shape: Make two full-size patterns of the chest ends (See *Layout: Chest Ends & End Build-ups* drawing, page 27) and mount these to ¼-in.-thick mahogany stock with spray adhesive. Band-saw the two chest ends to shape, cutting along the outside pattern layout lines only (**See Photo A**). Score along the pattern layout lines that mark the locations of the end build-ups with a utility knife and straightedge. Mark the line that will separate the lid ends from the box ends on these parts as well. Then peel off the paper patterns.

❷ Make the end build-ups. Rip and crosscut the two end build-up pieces from ½-in. stock. Cut a ¼-in.-wide, ⅛-in.-deep groove across the inside face of each build-up, ¼ in. up from the bottom edges of the parts. These grooves will house the chest bottom. Cut the two grooves on the table saw with a dado blade or on the router table with a ¼-in. straight bit.

❸ Attach the build-ups to the chest ends: Spread glue on the undadoed faces of the build-ups, align

Wood blade guide

PHOTO B: Glue the end build-ups to the chest ends, then clamp a wood blade guide to mark the location of the cutting line that separates the chest ends into the lid and box ends. Saw through the chest ends and build-ups with a back saw held against the wood blade guide.

them with the score marks on the chest ends, and clamp up the assemblies. The bottom edges of the parts should be held flush.

④ Cut through the chest end/build-up assemblies to separate the lid and box ends. A good way to do this is to clamp a block of wood along the lid/box separation line and use it as a blade guide for cutting through the parts with a back saw. Cut through the parts to produce two lid ends and two box ends (**See Photo B**).

BUILD THE LID

The arched chest lid is actually a combination of seven parts: the lid front, back, top, fillets and ends. You'll glue the parts together first, then trim off the square top front and back edges on the table saw and shape the arch with a hand plane and belt sander.

⑤ Cut the lid parts to size on the table saw: Rip and crosscut the lid top from ¾-in. stock. Bevel-rip, then crosscut the two lid fillets to size from ¾-in. stock as well. Cut the ½-in.-thick lid front and back pieces. For all of these parts, the grain should run lengthwise, to make planing easier.

⑥ Glue the lid parts together. Assemble the parts so the lid front, back and top fit around the build-ups on the lid ends. Spread glue on the square edges of the fillets, and clamp them into the inside corners of the lid (**See Photo C**).

⑦ Shape the top of the lid to conform with the lid end arcs. First, tilt your table saw blade to 45° and trim the long, square corners off the top of the lid before you begin planing. Doing so reduces

PHOTO C: Glue up the lid top, front, back and ends first, then reinforce the lid glue joints by attaching fillets to the long inside corners of the lid. Attach the fillets with glue and hold them in place with spring clamps.

PHOTO D: Trim off the long top corners of the lid on the table saw, with the blade tilted to 45°. Secure the lid in a bench vise and plane it to shape using the arcs on the lid ends as guides. Shave off the waste in long shallow passes with a sharp smoothing plane.

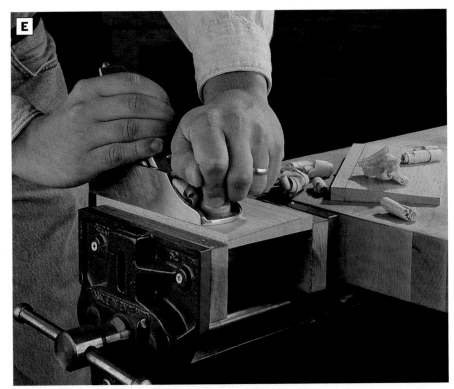

the amount of hand-planing you'll have to do. Clamp the lid in a bench vise, and plane the top, front and back of the lid until it conforms to the arched profiles of the lid ends. This process goes rather quickly and is easy to do on the soft mahogany. Work in long, smooth passes, planing with the grain (**See Photo D**). Stop planing when you are within about ¹⁄₁₆ in. of the lid end profiles, then finish shaping the lid with a belt sander and 150-grit paper.

ASSEMBLE THE BOX

The ends of the treasure chest box are wider at the top than at the bottom. You'll need to plane a taper into the box front and back pieces so they match the shape of the box ends, once the box is assembled. These workpieces are too thin and wide to form the tapers safely on the table saw or band saw, so you'll need to make them with a hand plane and sander instead.

8 Make the box front and back: Rip and crosscut these parts to size from ½-in. stock. Then refer to the *Layout: Chest Ends & End Build-ups* drawing, page 27, to mark both ends of the chest front and back workpieces for planing the tapered faces. Secure each workpiece in your bench vise, and follow the layout lines to shape the tapers with a hand plane (**See Photo E**). Once you've planed the tapers, flatten the planed surfaces with a belt sander. Then cut or rout ¼-in.-wide, ⅛-in.-deep grooves across the bottom inside faces of the chest front and back for the bottom panel. The grooves run the full length of these parts.

PHOTO E: Form tapers on the outside faces of the box front and back with a hand plane. Mark the profiles of the tapers on the ends of each workpiece. Remove the waste with a hand plane down to your layout lines, and sand the tapered areas smooth.

9 Cut the ¼-in.-thick bottom panel to size.

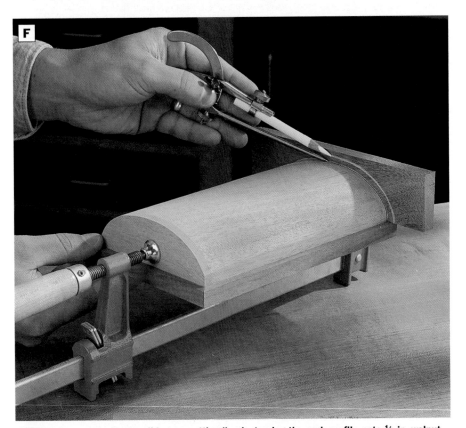

PHOTO F: Lay out the bottom lid strap cutting line by tracing the arch profile onto ½-in. walnut stock with a white colored pencil. Then scribe the top lid strap cutting line. Set the compass so the strapping will be ¼ in. thick. Draw layout lines all the way over the lid arch so the strapping will butt against the front and back walnut trim molding once it is cut and installed.

⑩ Glue and clamp the box together: Dry-assemble the box front and back between the box ends and against the build-ups. Fit the bottom panel into its grooves as well. Disassemble the parts, and sand the inside faces of the parts smooth. Then, spread glue on the ends of the front and back pieces as well as the ends of the build-ups, and clamp the box together with the bottom in place.

ADD THE DECORATIVE TRIM

⑪ Rip-cut two sticks of walnut for the straight trim pieces: Set the table saw fence ¼ in. from the blade, and rip three 2-ft. lengths for trim stock.

⑫ Cut the trim pieces to length: Crosscut the four front and back trim pieces as well as the four end pieces. Miter-cut the ends of these parts to 45°. Crosscut the four box straps to length. Sand the trim pieces smooth.

⑬ Install the straight trim. Glue and clamp the front and back trim and the box strapping to the lid and box. There's no need for nails.

⑭ Make the lid strapping. First, cut two 2 × 8-in. pieces of walnut to size. Clamp each walnut blank to the ends of the lid, and draw the lid profile on the walnut. Then, set a compass with a white colored pencil to ¼ in. and scribe around the lid onto the walnut to form the outer lid strapping cutting line (See Photo F). Cut out the lid strapping just outside your layout lines on the band saw or scroll saw. Sand the lid strapping on the drum sander until the pieces conform tightly to the lid curvature.

⑮ Glue the lid strapping in place on the lid.

FINISHING TOUCHES

⑯ Install the hinge. Start by paring a shallow mortise for the hinge into the back walnut trim of the lid and box with a sharp chisel. Drill tiny pilot holes for the hinge screws first, then attach the hinge to the box and lid.

⑰ Apply the finish. We decided to leave the mahogany and walnut wood tones natural, rather than wiping on a wood stain. Spray on three light coats of aerosol lacquer, available at craft stores. Buff between coats of finish with #0000 steel wool or 320-grit sandpaper to remove any grit and "burnish" the surface smooth.

⑱ Install the brass hook latch and ring pulls. Drill a pilot hole in the front lid and box trim for fastening the lid catch, and screw the catch in place. If you prefer, you could purchase and install a keyed jewelry box lock instead. For added charm, we attached a couple of decorative brass ring pulls on each end of the chest (See Photo G).

PHOTO G: Attach the brass hook latch and ring pulls to the chest. Be sure to drill pilot holes for the hook latch screws to keep them from splitting the front walnut trim pieces.

Shaker-style Keepsake Box

Shaker craftsmen created marvelous steam-bent oval boxes to store and organize such personal items as sewing kits, button collections and correspondence. Try your hand at steam-bending when you build our rendition of a Shaker-style box. Bending the ash parts of the box and lid is easier than it looks, thanks to an inexpensive steaming jig you can build yourself.

Vital Statistics: Shaker-style Keepsake Box

TYPE: Oval box with lid

OVERALL SIZE: Lid: 1⅛H by 4⅞W by 7⅛L
Box: 2⅜H by 4⅜W by 6⅞L

MATERIAL: Air-dried ash

JOINERY: Butt and rabbet joints

CONSTRUCTION DETAILS:

· Lid and box sides are bent from single pieces of ash
· Fingers on the lid and box sides are glued and finished with decorative brass pins
· Ash parts are made pliable by steaming in a plywood, shop-built steamer jig
· Sides of lid fit into a rabbet cut around the oval box top

FINISH: Wipe-on Danish oil

Building time

PREPARING STOCK
1-2 hours

LAYOUT
2-3 hours

CUTTING PARTS
2 hours

ASSEMBLY
2-3 hours

FINISHING
1 hour

TOTAL: 8-11 hours

Tools you'll use

· Table saw
· Band saw or scroll saw
· Clamps
· Drill/driver
· 2-in.-dia. hole saw
· Stationary belt sander
· Shop-built steamer jig (See page 36 for construction details)
· Large cooking pot and heat source (hotplate or stove)

Shopping list

☐ (1) ⅛ × 6 in. × 2 ft. air-dried (green) ash

☐ (1) ½ × 6 in. × 2 ft. ash

☐ (1) ¾ in. × 4 ft. × 8 ft. exterior plywood

☐ (1) 2-in.-dia. × 2 ft. heat-resistant hose

☐ #8 × 1½-in. galvanized deck screws

☐ (3) ⅜-in.-long brass pins

☐ Moisture-resistant and regular wood glue

☐ Finishing materials

Shaker-style Keepsake Box

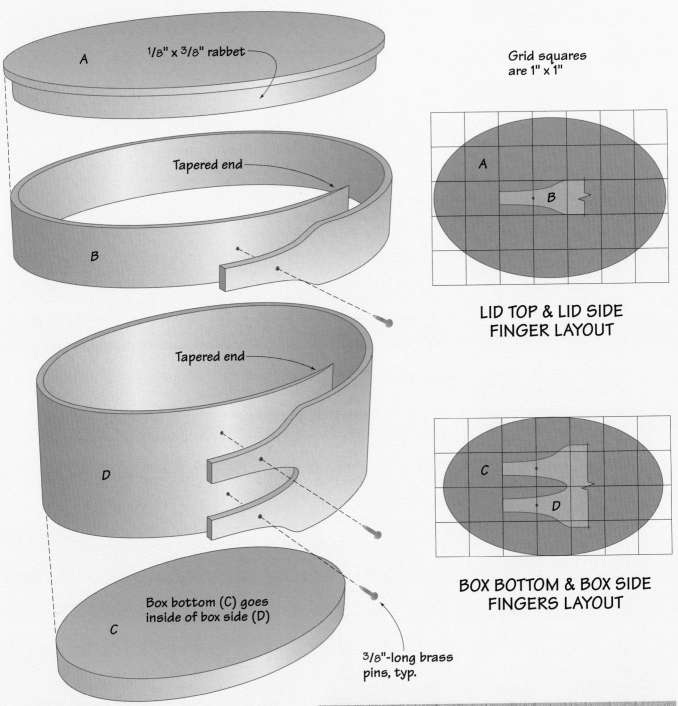

A

1/8" x 3/8" rabbet

Tapered end

B

Tapered end

D

C

Box bottom (C) goes
inside of box side (D)

3/8"-long brass
pins, typ.

Grid squares
are 1" x 1"

A

B

**LID TOP & LID SIDE
FINGER LAYOUT**

C

D

**BOX BOTTOM & BOX SIDE
FINGERS LAYOUT**

Shaker-style Keepsake Box Cutting List			
Part	**No.**	**Size**	**Material**
A. Lid top	1	1/2 × 4 7/8 × 7 1/8 in.	Ash
B. Lid side	1	1/8 × 1 × 24 in.	"
C. Box bottom	1	1/2 × 4 × 6 1/2 in.	"
D. Box side	1	1/8 × 2 3/8 × 24 in.	"

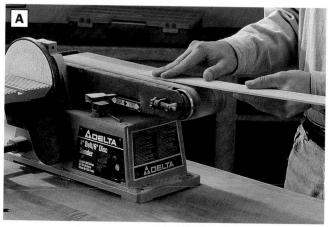

PHOTO A: The side pieces of both the lid and the box get tapered on one end to minimize the thickness of the overlap after they are bent to shape. Begin the taper about 2 in. in from one end of each part. A stationary belt sander works well for sanding these tapers.

MAKE THE LID & BOX SIDES

Some hardwoods are easier to bend than others. Ash is a good choice, as well as oak and cherry. Whatever species you choose, be sure it has been air-dried (often called "green") rather than kiln-dried. Kiln-drying destroys the elasticity of wood fibers and makes the wood prone to breaking when it bends. There's no way to tell, visually, if the stock has been air-dried, so ask your lumber supplier before you buy.

❶ Make the lid and box sides: Rip and crosscut the lid and box sides to size. You'll probably then need to resaw these workpieces on a band saw to reach the ⅛-in. thickness of the parts (See page 7). CAUTION: *If you need to resaw these parts, do your resawing first on a wider piece of ash, then rip and crosscut the parts to size. This way, you'll keep your fingers a safer distance from the blade during resawing.* Sand one end of each workpiece starting about 2 in. in and tapering to the end **(See Photo A)**. This taper will be necessary to compensate for the double thickness that results when the box sides overlap during assembly. Finally, use the *Finger Layout* drawings on page 34 to lay out and cut the fingers on the other ends of these parts. Sand the side pieces smooth.

BUILD A BENDING FORM

Once the thin ash parts are steamed, they must be clamped to an oval form immediately in order to form and retain their shape as they dry and cool. We built the plywood bending form shown in Photo B, right, which sandwiches the ash between an inner oval, made of four pieces of exterior plywood laminated together and screwed to a board, and two outer presses, also made of four plywood laminations. A pair of bar clamps squeeze the outer presses against the inner oval, holding the ash in shape.

❷ Build the bending form: Face-glue four 1 × 1-ft.

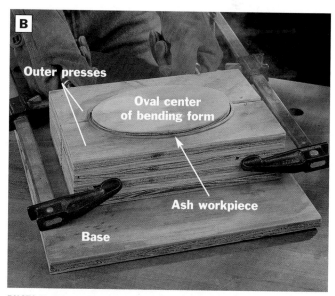

PHOTO B: Steam the ash workpiece until pliable, then remove it quickly from the steamer box and wrap it around the oval center of the bending form. Set the outer presses in place around the ash and clamp the presses together. Tighten the clamps so the ash conforms as closely as possible to the oval center of the bending form. Wear gloves when working with steamed wood—it will be extremely hot.

pieces of exterior plywood to form a 3-in.-thick blank. Lay out an oval in the center of the blank that matches the size of the box bottom (See *Box Bottom* drawing, page 34). Draw a line across the blank from edge to edge that splits the oval in half, lengthwise. On the band saw, cut along your centerlines up to the oval, then cut out the oval shape. The result is a thick oval as well as two waste pieces that become the two

Shop-built steamer jig

The steamer jig you'll need for this project is simply a long, narrow box made of exterior plywood with a 2-in.-dia. heat-resistant hose attached to one end and a hinged door on the other. A pot of boiling water supplies steam to the box through the hose, and the hose attaches to a plywood lid that covers the pot. As steam builds inside the jig, it surrounds the thin Shaker-box parts and softens them until they are pliable.

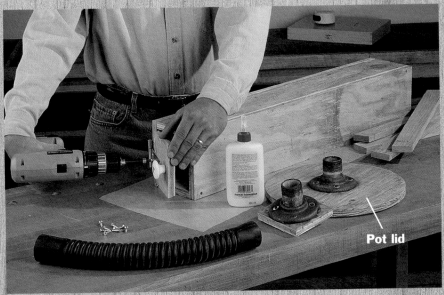

Construct the steamer jig from exterior-grade plywood, moisture-resistant wood glue and galvanized deck screws. Install a hinged door on one end of the steamer box, and drill a 2-in.-dia. hole in the other box end and the plywood pot lid for installing a length of heat-resistant or automotive radiator hose. Attach the hose to the steamer box and pot lid. We used metal fittings and threaded pipe for making these hose connections.

Attach a drain tube through a hole in the bottom of the jig near the door to let excess steam and condensed water vapor escape into a pail. Elevate your steamer on legs until it is higher than the pot to minimize bending the hose. This way, steam can rise and pass more easily into the box.

How to build the steamer jig

The proportions of the steamer box aren't critical, so long as there is space inside the box for the steam to make contact with the ash workpieces on all sides. We built our box from ¾-in. exterior-grade plywood and sized it 6 in. wide, 6 in. tall and 3 ft. long. Cut the top, bottom, sides, hose end and door to size. Cut four sticks for the steamer box legs and a round plywood lid to fit over the pot you'll use to boil water. Protect all surfaces that will face into the steamer box with a coat of exterior primer and paint. Use a hole saw to bore a 2-in.-dia. hole through the hose end of the box as well as the pot lid for the hose.

Attach the box sides and hose end to the box top and bottom pieces with moisture-resistant wood glue and 1½-in. galvanized deck screws. Install the door on the other end of the box with a galvanized hinge, and screw a knob to the door. Drill a ½-in.-dia. hole through the box bottom near the door for a drain tube. Then screw the legs to the steamer box.

Fasten the hose to the box end and to the pot lid. Car radiator hose works well for the tubing, but any 2-in.-dia. heat-resistant hose will do the trick. We used short lengths of threaded pipe attached to metal fittings to fasten the hose to the box end and pot lid. The hose ends friction-fit over the metal pipes. However you choose to fasten the hose, be sure the connections form a tight fit around the pot lid and steamer box holes.

Cut a handful of dowels or thin scrap sticks to 4-in. lengths; these will be used as spacers inside the steamer to keep the ash parts elevated off the box bottom so they'll steam evenly.

PHOTO C: Use a piloted rabbeting bit in the router table to mill the rabbet around the edges of the lid top. Hold the workpiece securely against the router table and bit with a foam-soled pushpad. Feed the workpiece around the bit clockwise to cut the rabbet.

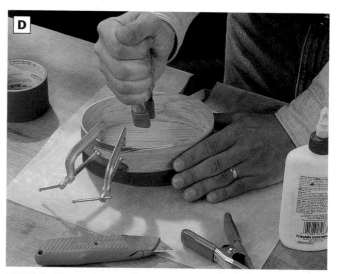

PHOTO D: Glue the side pieces to the box top and bottom. Hold the bentwood parts in position while the glue dries with strap, spring and C-clamps. Mask off the area around the fingers to protect these spots from glue squeeze-out.

outer presses. Trim off another ¼ in. of plywood along the curved edges of the outer presses to provide clearance for the bending stock. Belt-sand any irregularities on the cut edges of these three parts. Fasten the laminated oval to the center of a 2 × 2-ft. plywood base.

STEAM & BEND THE LID & BOX SIDES

❸ Set up your steaming jig (See *Steamer Jig*, previous page) and steam the lid and box side pieces. Plan to steam one workpiece at a time. Insert spacers beneath the ash part in the steamer box so the steam penetrates the workpiece from all sides. Insert the part and steam it for about 15 minutes until it is pliable. When the time is up, remove the workpiece and immediately wrap it around the oval center of the bending form, set the two outer presses in place and tighten the clamps (**See Photo B**). The ash will begin to cool and lose its flexibility almost instantly, so work quickly. Leave the workpiece clamped in the jig for two days so it dries thoroughly.

ASSEMBLE THE LID & BOTTOM

❹ Make the box top and bottom ovals: Lay out and cut the box top and bottom to size, according to the grid drawings on page 34. The lid sides fit into a ⅛-in.-deep, ⅜-in.-wide rabbet in the edge of the box top. Cut the rabbet with a piloted rabbeting bit in the router table (**See Photo C**). Sand these parts.

❺ Glue and clamp the bent ash parts to the box top and bottom. First, dry-fit the lid and box parts together with clamps, and mark the locations where the fingers overlap the sides. Release the clamps, and

PHOTO E: Drill pilot holes through the fingers on the lid and box sides, then tap the decorative brass pins into the pilot holes and against an anvil to flatten and bend over the pin tips inside the box.

apply masking tape along the outsides of the finger outlines. Then glue and clamp the bent wood parts to the box top and bottom ovals (**See Photo D**). When the glue stops squeezing out, remove the tape.

❻ Install the decorative brass pins: Drill a pilot hole through the fingers on the lid and box sides about 1 in. from the ends of the fingers. Tap the pins through the pilot holes and flatten them against an anvil inside the box (**See Photo E**).

❼ Finish the box by wiping on several coats of Danish oil. For a decorative touch, we covered the bottom of the box with a piece of felt.

This cutting board makes food preparation tasks easier, because it fits right over your sink basin where it's needed most. Build it from hard maple slats glued up "butcher-block" style to create a cutting surface that will stand up to years of hard use.

Over-sink
Cutting Board

Vital Statistics: Over-sink Cutting Board

TYPE: Cutting board

OVERALL SIZE: 15¼W by 1¼H by 17½L (You may need to modify overall length and width to accommodate the dimensions of your sink)

MATERIAL: Hard maple

JOINERY: Face-glued butt joints, screwed butt joints

CONSTRUCTION DETAILS:

· Board slats are oriented edge grain up, "butcher-block" style, to reduce wood movement and provide a more durable cutting surface

· Handle cutout and board edges rounded over

· Feet must be cut to fit your sink basin, then attached with screws beneath the cutting board

FINISH: Butcher block or mineral oil

Building time

 PREPARING STOCK
2 hours

 LAYOUT
1 hour

 CUTTING PARTS
3-4 hours

 ASSEMBLY
1 hour

 FINISHING
1 hour

TOTAL: 8-9 hours

Tools you'll use

· Planer
· Jointer
· Table saw
· Clamps
· Router with ¼-in. piloted roundover bit
· Drill/driver or drill press
· Jig saw
· Files and rasps
· Belt sander

Shopping list

☐ (1) 4/4 hard maple, about 8 board ft.

☐ #8 × 1½-in. stainless-steel flathead wood screws

☐ Polyurethane glue

☐ Two-part epoxy

☐ Finishing materials

Over-sink Cutting Board

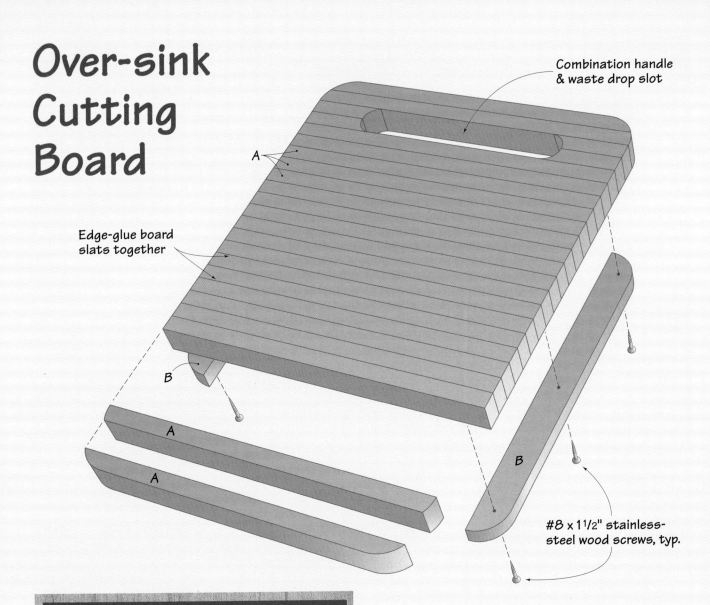

Combination handle & waste drop slot

A

Edge-glue board slats together

B

A

A

B

#8 x 1½" stainless-steel wood screws, typ.

Over-sink Cutting Board Cutting List

Part	No.	Size	Material
A. Board slats	23	¾ × 1¼ × 15¾* in.	Hard maple
B. Feet	2	¾ × 1½ × 16* in.	"

* Length will vary, depending on sink dimensions

Adjust overall dimensions & feet locations so cutting board fits your sink

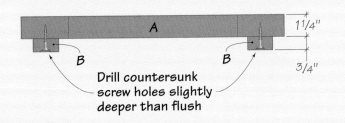

A

1¼"

B

B

3/4"

Drill countersunk screw holes slightly deeper than flush

END VIEW

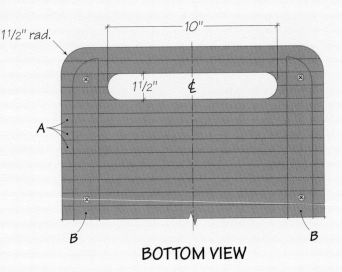

1½" rad.

10"

1½"

₵

A

B

B

BOTTOM VIEW

MAKE THE BOARD SLATS

❶ Plane the 4/4 maple stock to ¾ in. thick (See page 7). Then joint one long edge smooth and flat. When planing hard maple, remove no more than 1/32 in. with each pass to keep from prematurely dulling the planer knives.

❷ Cut the slats to length and width. First crosscut the maple into 15¾-in.-long blanks. Then set your table saw's fence 1¼-in. from the blade. With the jointed edge of the boards against the fence, rip-cut each blank into slats (See Photo A). Cut 23 slats in all.

GLUE UP THE SLATS

❸ When gluing up this cutting board, you could glue and clamp all the joints at once, but it would be difficult to tighten the clamps without the slats sliding out of alignment with one another in the process. A better method is to glue up half the slats in one assembly, glue up the other half in a second assembly, then join the halves with one final glue joint when the halves are dry. You'll also be able to run these narrower glued-up assemblies through a power planer to smooth them.

❹ Glue up 12 slats: Place a sheet of wax paper on a flat workbench to protect the bench from glue squeeze-out. Apply an even coat-

PHOTO A: Crosscut the maple stock to 15¾-in. blanks, then rip the blanks into 1¼-in.-wide slats on the table saw. You'll need to make 23 of these slats for the cutting board.

PHOTO B: Glue and clamp the slats into groups of 12 and 11, then join these two subassemblies together to form the full cutting board blank. Subassemblies make final clamp-up easier.

ing of moisture-resistant wood glue to the mating faces of each slat, and clamp up the assembly. You could also use polyurethane glue for even more water resistance, but be sure to dampen one surface of each glue joint with water first, before applying the glue. (Polyurethane glue requires moisture in order to set up.) Alternate clamps above and below the slats to distribute clamping pressure evenly over the width of the assembly. Tighten the clamps just enough to close the glue joints. Use a mallet to tap the slats flat if they shift out of alignment.

PHOTO C: Trim the ends of the board on the table saw to even up the slats and establish the final length of the cutting board. Ours was 15½ in., but yours might vary, depending on your sink.

PHOTO D: Mark for the 1½-in. radius corners, and cut the corners to shape with a jig saw. Then smooth all of the edges with a belt sander.

5 Glue up the remaining 11 slats as you did in Step 4. Both slat glue-ups can occur at the same time if you have enough clamps.

6 Plane both faces of each slat assembly to even out the edges of the slats and remove all glue squeeze-out. Be sure to plane both assemblies at the same planer thickness settings to achieve two panels that are the same final thickness. A few shallow passes on each face should be all you'll need to produce flat, smooth faces.

7 Glue and clamp the two slat subassemblies together to form the full cutting board blank (**See Photo B**).

8 Trim the ends of the board on the table saw to cut the blank to final length (**See Photo C**). Let the final cutting board length be determined by the size of your sink. The board should completely overlap the sink opening and rest fully on the sink rim.

9 Round the corners of the board to shape: Use a compass to draw the 1½-in. radius on each corner, and trim the corners to rough shape with a jig saw. Then finish the arcs with a belt sander (**See Photo D**). Belt-sand the edges, ends, and faces of the board now, to remove any remaining saw and planer marks.

10 Cut out the handle: Lay out the proportions and location of the handle, using the *Bottom View* drawing on page 40 as a guide. At the drill press, bore out the ends of the handle with a 1½-in. bit. Then use a jig saw to cut the straight lines that connect the large holes and complete the handle (**See Photo E**). If you don't have a drill press, you could also drill an entry hole for the jig saw blade and make the complete handle cutout with the jig saw instead.

11 Smooth the board edges: Round over the edges of the handle cutout and the top and bottom edges of the board with a router and ¼-in. piloted roundover bit.

INSTALL THE FEET

12 Make and install the feet: Rip and crosscut two lengths of maple for the feet, with the lengths sized according to the inside opening of your sink basin. Carefully mark the foot locations on the cutting board, so the feet run perpendicular to the slats and are flush with the sink basin walls. TIP: *Use short strips of double-sided carpet tape to hold the feet in place when you are determining their final placement on the cutting board. This way, you can shift the foot positions as needed to achieve the best fit on the sink before installing with screws.* Drill countersunk pilot holes through the feet and into the board, and install the feet with two-part epoxy and 1½-in. stainless-steel or brass wood screws **(See Photo F)**.

FINISHING TOUCHES

13 Rub several coats of a food-safe finish, like butcher block or mineral oil, on all exposed surfaces of the cutting board. Pay special attention to end-grain areas, such as around the handle and on the board ends; these spots are especially susceptible to water absorption and damage. Once it dries, a food-safe finish will not seal the board entirely. For that reason, never submerse the board in water, and wipe the board dry after washing it clean. Do not clean in a dishwasher.

PHOTO E: Make the handle cutout by first drilling the curved ends with a 1½-in. bit or hole saw. Cut out the remaining waste with a jig saw, and clean up the edges with a file.

PHOTO F: Cut the feet to size and shape. Then set the cutting board in place on your sink to determine the best positions for the feet. Mark the locations of the feet on the board. Attach the feet with stainless-steel flathead wood screws and two-part epoxy.

Knife Storage Block

One of the most useful accessories in any cook's repertoire, a solid-wood knife block keeps blades safely at hand and neatly stored while protecting their sharpened edges. This knife block is sized to fit on countertops beneath wall cabinets, and it's easy to build. Slots for the knives are simply dadoed into one face of each strip before assembly. The knife block is made of beech, a tough, beautiful wood commonly used for kitchen accessories.

Vital Statistics: Knife Storage Block

TYPE: Knife block

OVERALL SIZE: $7\frac{5}{8}$W by $8\frac{5}{8}$H by $10\frac{3}{4}$L

MATERIAL: Beech

JOINERY: Face-glued laminations, butt joints reinforced with screws

CONSTRUCTION DETAILS:
· Slots for knives are cut into one face of the block laminations to make alignment easy during glue-up
· Can be built with standard ¾-in.-thick stock if you choose to use a more common hardwood, like maple, for this project
· Block designed to hide the bottom open ends of the knife slots
· Legs fasten to the block with screws

FINISH: Clear satin polyurethane

Building time

PREPARING STOCK
2 hours

LAYOUT
1 hour

CUTTING PARTS
2 hours

ASSEMBLY
1 hour

FINISHING
1 hour

TOTAL: 7 hours

Tools you'll use

· Table saw
· Planer
· Jointer
· Band saw, scroll saw or jig saw
· Drill/driver
· Clamps

Shopping list

☐ (8) ⁴⁄₄ × 4 in. × 10 ft. beech
☐ (1) ⁴⁄₄ × 6 in. × 2 ft. beech
☐ #8 × 1¼-in. flathead wood screws
☐ Moisture-resistant wood glue
☐ Finishing materials

PREPARE THE STRIPS

❶ Plane all of the 4/4 beech stock down to ¾ in. thick. Beech is an excellent choice for this project, as its tight grain will resist warping. Choose quartersawn stock if possible, which is less likely to expand and contract dramatically in response to changes in humidity. Be sure the faces of the stock are flat.

❷ Rip stock for the strips to width. Make these rip cuts on the table saw with the blade set to 3½ in., then flatten and smooth the cut edges on the jointer.

❸ Crosscut 10 strips to length. Lay out the groove locations on the strips using the *End View Block Laminations* drawing on page 47 as a guide. The widths and depths of these dado cuts will vary, depending on the dimensions of your knife blades.

❹ Mill grooves into the strips. Make these cuts with either a dado head in your table saw or a straight bit and fence on a router table (**See Photo A**). If you want to include a hole for holding a sharpening rod, cut a square groove for it now, along with the rest of the knife slots.

❺ Lay out and cut the angled ends on each of the strips, according to the dimensions given on the *Side View Block Laminations* drawing, page 47. Cut these angles on the table saw with the miter gauge set to 45° (**See Photo B**). Cut away the larger angled portion first, then reset the miter gauge to 45° in the opposite direction to nibble away the smaller angle.

SHAPE THE FEET

❻ Lay out and cut the two feet to shape: Cut blanks for the feet to 8 in. long and 5 in. wide, with the grain running lengthwise. Draw a 1 × 1-in. grid onto one workpiece, and draw the *Side View Feet* profile shown on page 47 onto the blank. Trim this leg to shape on a

PHOTO A: Cut the knife slots into one face of the strips using a dado blade on the table saw (as shown), or on a router table with a straight bit and fence.

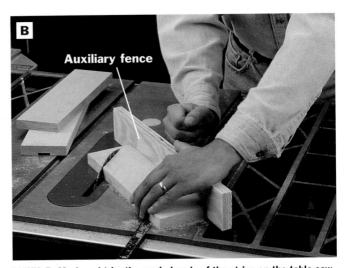

PHOTO B: Mark and trim the angled ends of the strips on the table saw with workpieces supported by the miter gauge set to a 45° angle. Attach a piece of scrap to the miter gauge to serve as an auxiliary fence. Doing so provides better workpiece support and control.

band saw, scroll saw or with a jig saw (**See Photo C**). Use the leg as a pattern for tracing the profile onto the second leg blank, and cut it to shape. Then clamp the legs together and gang-sand them on the drum sander so they match.

GLUE UP THE BLOCK

❼ Keeping glue out of the knife grooves will be your biggest challenge when gluing up so many strips at once. Here's a solution to help remedy the problem: Cut strips of ⅛-in.-thick scrap wood to fill each knife

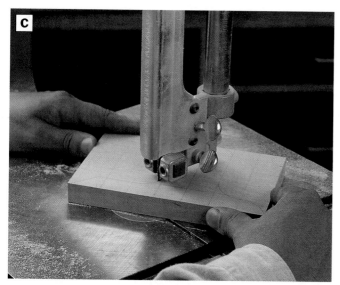

PHOTO C: Lay out and cut one foot to shape on the band saw. Use this workpiece as a template for drawing and cutting the second leg to shape. Then clamp the legs together and sand both smooth at one time.

PHOTO D: After your clamps have squeezed the excess glue from the assembly, but before the glue starts to set, remove the wax-coated filler strips in the knife slots. Once the glue dries, sand the block smooth.

slot dado. Make these pieces fit snugly but not tightly. They should be able to slide easily into and out of the dadoes when the block is clamped together. Coat each filler strip with paraffin wax to repel glue.

8 Dry-fit the 10 strips together and temporarily clamp them. Check to be sure that all the knives fit into their grooves. They should be loose enough to facilitate easy removal, yet snug enough so the fit isn't sloppy. You may even want to mark the configuration of the strips so they'll be easy to organize once you start the gluing process.

9 Glue and clamp the strips together. First, spread an even coat of glue onto both faces of the inner 8 strips and on the inside face of the two outside strips. Then set the waxed filler strips into the knife slots. NOTE: *Apply a thin, even coating of glue. The strips will be more likely to slip out of alignment when you clamp them if the glue is too thick, because it will act like a lubricant.* Assemble the block laminations into a block. Alternate bar or pipe clamps above and below the block to distribute clamping pressure evenly, and gradually tighten the clamps until the joints between the laminations just close. Tap the workpieces with a mallet, if necessary, to keep the edges and ends even. Wipe up glue squeeze-out with a wet rag, and remove the filler strips before the glue has a chance to set to keep the strips from sticking (**See Photo D**).

10 Sand the block thoroughly after the glue has dried to remove all traces of excess glue, working your way up to 220-grit paper.

FINISHING TOUCHES

11 Install the legs on the block: Drive 1¼-in. flathead wood screws through countersunk pilot holes in the legs and into the block to attach the parts. Align the parts so the bottom front corners of the legs are even with the bottom end of the block (**See Photo E**).

12 Seal the block with several coats of clear polyurethane varnish. Or leave the block natural if you prefer.

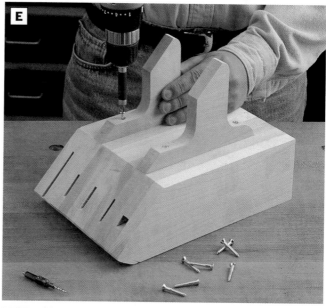

PHOTO E: Drive flathead wood screws through the feet and into the bottom of the knife block. Drill countersunk pilot holes for the screws first, to make screw installation easier and to recess the screw heads.

Domino Set

Somewhere around 1720, dominoes found their way to Europe by way of the silk route from China. Sets dating back some 600 years earlier have been discovered in Eastern Asia. But the game most of us know as "Dominoes" is an American version with its roots in the early 20th century. Also known as Muggins or Five-up, the basic game requires just 28 tiles. Follow our project plans to build a set of handmade walnut and maple dominoes, along with a handy storage box.

Vital Statistics: Domino Set

TYPE: Dominoes and box

OVERALL SIZE: Dominoes: 1W by $^{11}/_{32}$H by 2L
Storage box: 5¼W by 1⅝H by 8¼L

MATERIAL: Walnut, self-stick maple veneer, Plexiglas

JOINERY: Laminated butt joints, miters and dadoes

CONSTRUCTION DETAILS:
- Maple veneer and walnut emulate traditional ivory and ebony dominoes
- Several simple shop jigs are employed to improve accuracy and safety when machining small domino tiles
- Drilling through the maple veneer produces walnut-colored dots on the dominoes
- Storage box outfitted with a sliding lid

FINISH: Satin polyurethane varnish

Building time

 PREPARING STOCK
2 hours

 LAYOUT
3-4 hours

 CUTTING PARTS
2 hours

 ASSEMBLY
4-5 hours

 FINISHING
1 hour

TOTAL: 12-14 hours

Tools you'll use

- Table saw
- Jointer
- Power miter saw (optional)
- Drill press with ³/₁₆-in. twist bit
- Frame clamp

Shopping list

- ☐ (1) ¹/₄₀ in. × 2 ft. × 2 ft. self-stick maple veneer
- ☐ (2) ¼ × 2 in. × 3 ft. walnut
- ☐ (1) ½ × 2 in. × 3 ft. walnut
- ☐ (1) ¼ × 6 × 12-in. birch plywood
- ☐ (1) ⅛ × 4½ × 7⅞ in. Plexiglas
- ☐ Wood glue
- ☐ Finishing materials

MAKE THE DOMINO BLANKS

To replicate the look of ivory tiles with inlaid ebony dots, adhere two strips of self-stick maple veneer onto a walnut core, then drill through the veneer on one face of each domino to expose the walnut beneath, producing patterns of dots on the maple.

❶ Rip-cut the ¼-in. walnut stock to 1 in. wide for the domino cores: To make a standard set of 28 dominoes, start with two 36-in.-long strips of 1-in.-wide walnut, which will provide enough material for making a few extra dominoes in case of errors. Since the long walnut edges of each domino will show, remove any saw kerf marks left on the edges of the walnut by running the strips on edge over a jointer.

❷ Apply the maple veneer to both faces of the long walnut strips: Peel off the protective paper that covers the veneer's adhesive backing and press the veneer firmly into place on the walnut. To make most efficient use of the veneer, align the edge of the veneer sheet with the edge of each walnut strip when you bond the two together. Then trim the veneer cleanly along the edge of the walnut with a sharp utility knife (**See Photo A**).

❸ Crosscut the domino tiles to length. Clamp a stop-block to the fence of a power miter saw, 2 in. from the blade, and cut the long walnut and maple strips into as many 2-in. domino tiles as you can (**See Photo B**). To minimize tearing out the wood, install a sharp carbide-tipped crosscut blade or plywood-cutting blade in the saw to make these cuts.

CUT THE CENTERLINES

❹ Cut centerlines across one face of each domino. Make these cuts on the table saw. Since the tiles are too small to hold against the miter gauge safely by hand, you'll need to build a simple jig to hold the

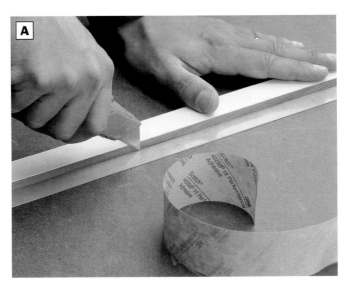

PHOTO A: Peel off the protective paper that covers the adhesive backing of the maple veneer and adhere it to the ¼-in.-thick walnut strips. Trim the veneer to fit the walnut with a sharp utility knife.

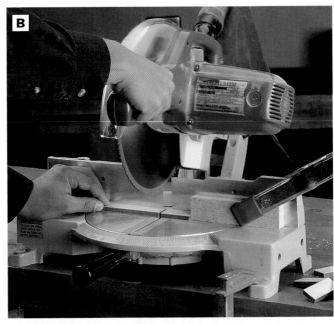

PHOTO B: Crosscut the laminated strips into individual domino tiles using a stopblock clamped to the fence of a power miter saw. Set the block 2 in. from the blade, and cut the dominoes one after the next.

dominoes in place while you cut them. The jig consists of a hold-down made from a piece of ¾-in.-wide scrap with a notch cut along one edge. Screw the hold-down to an auxiliary fence on the miter gauge. The notch should face the saw table and be just large enough to hold one domino at a time securely against the saw table. Set your table saw blade height so the blade will just trim through the veneer layer on the domino. Practice on a spare domino first, so you are sure the hold-down is attached accurately to the miter gauge. Then cut the centerlines one by one, slipping a domino blank into the hold-down and sliding the miter gauge over the saw blade (**See Photo C**). Cut a centerline across one face of each domino tile only.

MARK & DRILL THE DOTS

5 Lay out the dot patterns on your dominoes. See the full-size domino and dot patterns shown on page 53 for layout guides. To make locating the dots easier, we used the printed pattern to make a marking template from clear Plexiglas. We drilled $\frac{1}{16}$-dia. holes through the plastic at each dot and mounted the Plexiglas template to a wood jig, sized to hold one domino. We marked for the dots by pressing a finish nail through the appropriate holes in the template and into the maple veneer (**See Photo D**).

6 Drill the dots: Install a $\frac{3}{16}$-in.-dia. twist bit in the drill press, and clamp a fence to the drill press table.

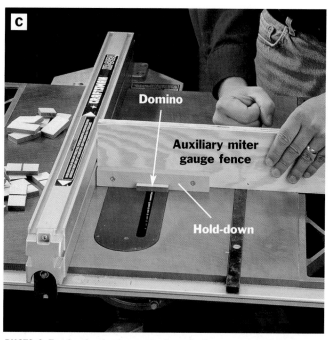

PHOTO C: To trim the domino centerlines, fasten a notched hold-down to an auxiliary fence mounted on the table saw miter gauge. The hold-down keeps your hands a safe distance from the blade and aligns each domino accurately to make the shallow centerline cut. Cut a centerline across one face of each domino.

PHOTO D: Mark the dot locations on the domino blanks, using the *Tile Holes & Centerlines* pattern drawing on page 53 as a guide. For greater precision, we built a simple jig with a clear Plexiglas top drilled with $\frac{1}{16}$-in.-dia. holes at each dot location. We pressed a finish nail through the appropriate holes in the Plexiglas to mark each dot pattern.

PHOTO E: Drill shallow holes through the maple veneer and just into the walnut core to create the domino dots. Set the depth stop to keep the bit from drilling too deeply. Clamp a fence to the drill press table so the rows of dots will line up lengthwise along the dominoes. Work carefully when drilling to hit your dot locations precisely.

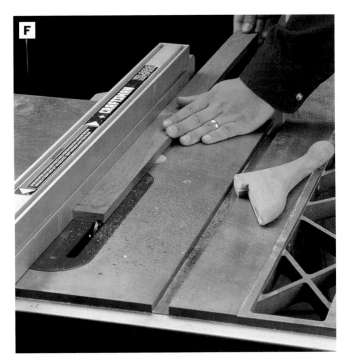

PHOTO F: Cut the ¼-in-wide groove for the box bottom using a dado blade in the table saw. Then install a ⅛-in.-kerfed blade in the saw and cut a groove for the sliding lid along the opposite long edge of the workpiece. Cutting these grooves now allows you to work more safely with a long workpiece and ensures that the grooves will align perfectly when you assemble the box later.

PHOTO G: Cut the box sides and ends to length. We set a power miter saw to 45° so that the parts would be both cut to length and also mitered for assembly. Accuracy is especially critical if you perform both of these operations in one step.

(A twist bit is a better choice for drilling the dots than a brad-point bit because it produces a smooth-bottomed hole without leaving a spur mark.) Align the fence for boring the center row of dots first. When drilling the dots, bring the tip of the drill bit down until it just touches the veneer and makes a tiny dimple on the wood. Do not pierce the veneer. Use this depression as a guide to shift the domino until the bit hits your dot mark. Set the depth stop on the drill press so that the bit goes through the top (maple) layer and barely enters the middle (walnut) core. Once the center rows of dots are drilled, reset the fence to drill the two outside rows of dots, and drill these dots on all of the dominoes **(See Photo E)**. (NOTE: *You don't need to change the fence setting in order to drill both outside rows. Just flip the dominoes end-for-end.*)

MAKE THE BOX

7 Cut the plywood box bottom to size.

8 Rip a 30-in. length of ½-in.-thick walnut stock to 1⅝ in. wide for the box sides and ends. Then set up a ¼-in.-wide dado blade in your table saw to plow the groove for the box bottom. Make a test cut on some scrap and check the fit of the plywood bottom in the groove (some ¼-in. plywood is quite a bit shy of its nominal thickness). Then plow the groove ⅛ in. from one long edge of the workpiece **(See Photo F)**.

9 Cut a ⅛-in.-wide groove ⅛ in. in from the other long edge of the walnut box workpiece for the sliding lid. Here, the groove should be slightly wider than the Plexiglas is thick; you want the top to be able to slide freely, but not loosely. Test-fit the Plexiglas box lid in the groove; if it barely slides with the protective film in place, it will be a good fit once the film is removed (don't remove it yet).

10 Miter-cut the box sides, front and back to length. A power miter saw works best for this operation, but you could make these cuts on a table saw as well. Since the 45° miter cuts will serve as the cuts that mark the length of the parts, measure carefully when you cut the angles **(See Photo G)**.

11 Dry-fit the box sides and ends. Check the fit of the miter joints and sand the joints, if needed, to improve the fit.

12 Trim the box front to 1¼ in. wide along the lid edge. The cut will trim off the lid groove on this part.

This way, the lid will slide over the box front once the box is assembled. Then glue up the miter joints and clamp the box together with the bottom inserted in the ¼-in. groove (**See Photo H**).

⓭ Sand the edges and ends of the Plexiglas lid with emory or wet/dry sandpaper, and drill a 1-in.-dia. hole 1¼ in. from one end to serve as a finger catch. Drill the hole with a sharp bit on the drill press at a slow speed to keep the plastic from cracking or chipping.

⓮ Sand the entire project with 220-grit paper, and round the corners of the dominoes. Then apply three coats of clear satin polyurethane varnish to all wood surfaces. Spray-on polyurethane works well for finishing these small parts.

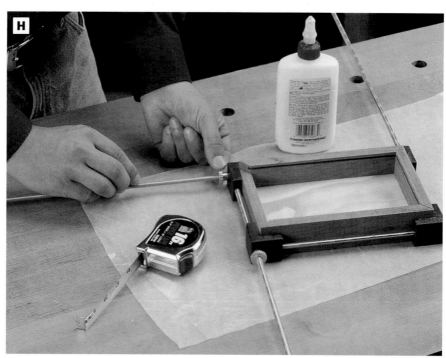

PHOTO H: Glue and clamp the box parts together, with the box bottom in place. We used a frame clamp, which holds all four corners of the box together and squares up the assembly as well. If you use a different clamping method, adjust the clamps until the box is square.

Dominoes rules of play

The most common game of dominoes is called Five-up, Muggins or sometimes All-Fives. It is played with the standard double-six set of 28 dominoes you've just made in this project. Two to four people can play, and you should have a pen and paper handy to track their individual scores.

Turn all the dominoes facedown on a flat surface. Each player then takes a tile (also known as a bone) to see who goes first. The one with the most dots starts, and the order of play goes clockwise around the table. Each player draws five tiles from the pile after returning the initial ones to the pile and shuffling the tiles around.

The first player can play any tile to get things started. The next player must then match either end of that tile (for example, if the initial tile has a four and a five, the second player can butt a four to the four or a five to the five).

When someone plays a double (with the same number of dots on each side of the line), this is placed crosswise at the end of the chain. Up to four dominoes can butt against this double: two continuing the chain in its original direction, and two more leading off at right angles.

If a player doesn't have a play to make, he or she must continue to draw tiles and keep them until a play can be made. A player can also decide against playing a tile he or she already has, in order to draw from the pile instead.

Points are awarded as a round progresses to players who form unions of tiles that total up to a multiple of five. However, a player only gets the points if he or she claims them before the next player takes a turn.

The first player to use up all of his or her tiles scores points from the tiles that remain in the other players' piles. These totals are rounded off to the nearest five (round 2 down and 3 up). If play comes to a stop because nobody has a playable domino, all the players add up their remaining tiles. The player with the lowest total scores points from the tiles that remain in all the other players' piles.

There are numerous variations of these rules, and no hard and fast "right" way to play. Several versions can be found in books on games at your local library or through searches on the Internet. Individual families, clubs or social groups often have "house" rules, too.

Collapsible Band Saw Basket

This ingenious gift, which imitates an Irish folk-art design, makes a handy table accent piece. The basket is formed by cutting a series of concentric spirals in a wide piece of stock with the band saw table set at an angle. These angled spiral cuts allow the center of the basket to drop down into a tapered bowl shape or collapse flat for storage.

Vital Statistics: Collapsible Band Saw Basket

TYPE: Collapsible basket

OVERALL SIZE: 9⁵⁄₁₆W by 9½D by 12⅜L

MATERIAL: Red oak

JOINERY: None

CONSTRUCTION DETAILS:

· Can be made from 1 board ft. of ¾-in. hardwood
· Basket spiral cuts are made on the band saw with the table tilted to 3°
· Basket and stand pivot open on screws
· Project folds flat for storage (See bottom photo)

FINISH: Satin polyurethane varnish

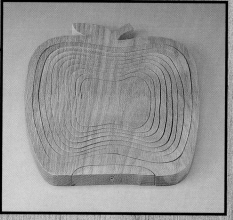

Building time

PREPARING STOCK
½ hour

LAYOUT
½ hour

CUTTING PARTS
1 hour

ASSEMBLY
½ hour

FINISHING
½ hour

TOTAL: 3 hours

Tools you'll use

· Planer and jointer (optional)
· Band saw with ³⁄₁₆-in. scrolling blade
· Drill/driver
· Belt sander
· Band clamp

Shopping list

☐ (1) ¾ × 10 in. × 2 ft. red oak
or
(2) ¾ × 5 in. × 2 ft. red oak

☐ (2) #6 × ¾-in. brass screws

☐ (1) #6 × 1-in. brass screw

☐ Wood glue

☐ Finishing materials

Cedar Bird Feeder

Invite songbirds into your yard or garden with this aromatic cedar bird feeder. Our design features a wide, protective roof to keep the feed dry, along with narrow perches to discourage larger predator birds. The feeder can be mounted to a post or hung from a branch, and you can build one in an afternoon.

Vital Statistics: Cedar Bird Feeder

TYPE: Bird feeder

OVERALL SIZE: 6W by 9¾H by 8L

MATERIAL: Aromatic cedar

JOINERY: Miters, screwed butt joints

CONSTRUCTION DETAILS:

· Lid hinges open on one side for cleaning and filling

· Plexiglas end panels are epoxied into shallow grooves in the sides

· Perches made of ¼-in. doweling

· Part ends are rounded over for finished look

FINISH: None

Building time

PREPARING STOCK
1 hour

LAYOUT
1 hour

CUTTING PARTS
2 hours

ASSEMBLY
2 hours

FINISHING
None

TOTAL: 6 hours

Tools you'll use

· Table saw

· Drill/driver

· Power miter saw (optional)

· Clamps

· Router table with ⅜-in. roundover bit

· Belt sander (optional)

· Drill press

· Hammer and nailset

Shopping list

☐ (1) ¾ × 6 in. × 4 ft. aromatic cedar

☐ (2) ⅛ × 3½ × 5⅞ in. Plexiglas

☐ ¼-in.-dia. hardwood dowel

☐ Two-part epoxy

☐ 4d galvanized finish nails

☐ ¾ × 4-in. brass jewelry box hinge

☐ Polyurethane glue

This project proves that some toys simply aren't for kids. With its walnut case, delicate moldings and brass hardware, this chessboard project will be the perfect complement to your cherished chess set. Our design features a pair of drawers for storing chess pieces during and after a game, and the walnut-and-maple checkered top is easier to build than you might think.

Double-drawer Chessboard

Vital Statistics: Cedar Bird Feeder

TYPE: Bird feeder

OVERALL SIZE: 6W by 9¾H by 8L

MATERIAL: Aromatic cedar

JOINERY: Miters, screwed butt joints

CONSTRUCTION DETAILS:

- Lid hinges open on one side for cleaning and filling
- Plexiglas end panels are epoxied into shallow grooves in the sides
- Perches made of ¼-in. doweling
- Part ends are rounded over for finished look

FINISH: None

Building time

PREPARING STOCK
1 hour

LAYOUT
1 hour

CUTTING PARTS
2 hours

ASSEMBLY
2 hours

FINISHING
None

TOTAL: 6 hours

Tools you'll use

- Table saw
- Drill/driver
- Power miter saw (optional)
- Clamps
- Router table with ⅜-in. roundover bit
- Belt sander (optional)
- Drill press
- Hammer and nailset

Shopping list

- ☐ (1) ¾ × 6 in. × 4 ft. aromatic cedar
- ☐ (2) ⅛ × 3½ × 5⅞ in. Plexiglas
- ☐ ¼-in.-dia. hardwood dowel
- ☐ Two-part epoxy
- ☐ 4d galvanized finish nails
- ☐ ¾ × 4-in. brass jewelry box hinge
- ☐ Polyurethane glue

Cedar Bird Feeder

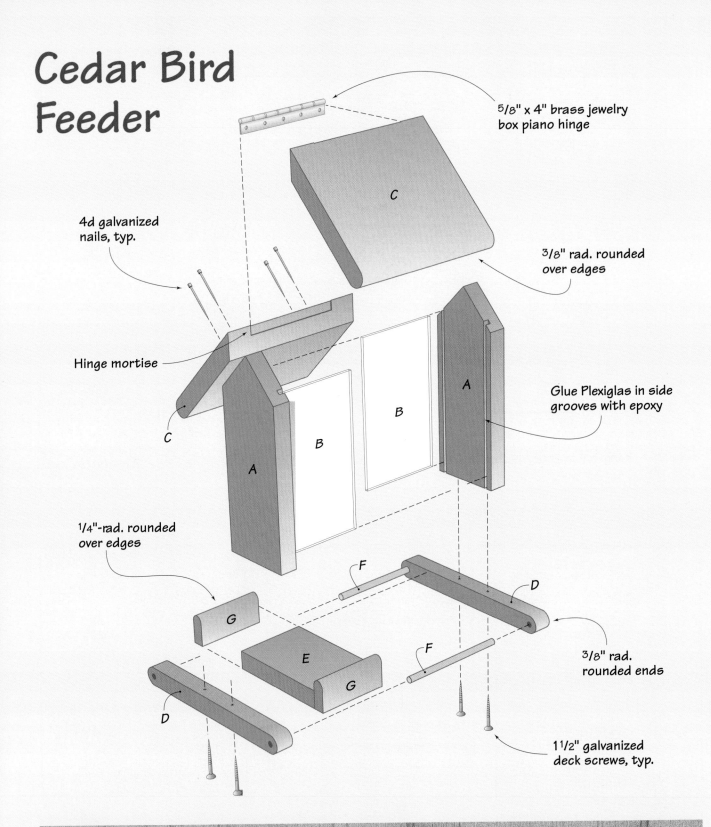

5/8" x 4" brass jewelry box piano hinge

4d galvanized nails, typ.

3/8" rad. rounded over edges

Hinge mortise

Glue Plexiglas in side grooves with epoxy

1/4"-rad. rounded over edges

3/8" rad. rounded ends

1 1/2" galvanized deck screws, typ.

Cedar Bird Feeder Cutting List

Part	No.	Size	Material
A. Sides	2	3/4 × 3 × 8 in.	Cedar
B. Ends	2	1/8 × 3 1/2 × 5 7/8 in.	Plexiglas
C. Roof panels	2	3/4 × 6 × 5 1/8 in.	Cedar
D. Base strips	2	3/4 × 3/4 × 8 in.	"

Part	No.	Size	Material
E. Base plate	1	3/4 × 3 × 4 1/2 in.	Cedar
F. Perches	2	1/4-in.-dia. × 4 1/2 in.	Hardwood dowel
G. Feed dams	2	1/2 × 1 1/4 × 3 in.	Cedar

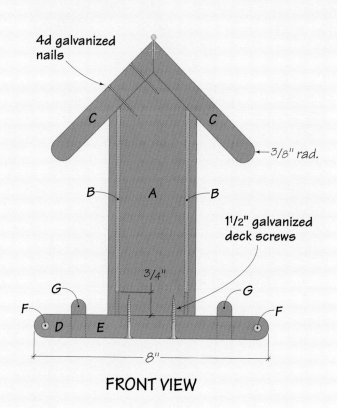

4d galvanized nails

C   C

3/8" rad.

B   A   B

1 1/2" galvanized deck screws

3/4"

G   G

F   D   E   F

8"

FRONT VIEW

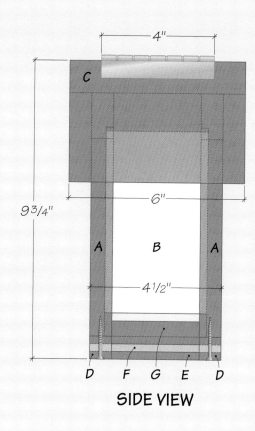

4"

C

9 3/4"

6"

A   B   A

4 1/2"

D   F   G   E   D

SIDE VIEW

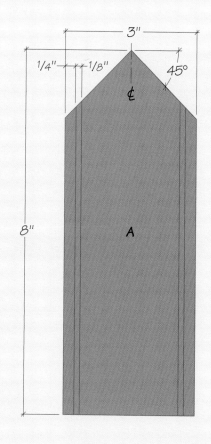

3"

1/4"   1/8"   45°

₵

8"

A

FRONT VIEW SIDES

1/4" rad.

1 1/4"   G

1/2"

END VIEW FEED DAMS

1/4"   A   3/4"

TOP VIEW SIDES

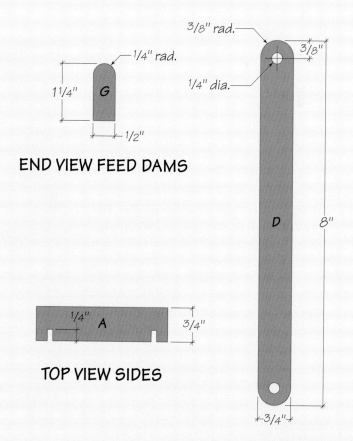

3/8" rad.

3/8"

1/4" dia.

D

8"

3/4"

FRONT VIEW BASE STRIPS

Cedar Bird Feeder **67**

MAKE THE SIDES & ENDS

1 Lay out and cut the two sides to shape: Rip stock for the sides to 3 in. wide, and crosscut the workpieces to 8 in. long. Form gables on one end of each side panel at the power miter saw with the blade turned 45° to the right or left **(See Photo A)**. You can also make these gable cuts on the table saw with each workpiece held against the miter gauge, set at 45°. Align the cuts so the tip of the gable is centered on the width of the sides.

2 Cut grooves in the sides for the Plexiglas end panels. See the *Front View Sides* drawing on page 67 for positioning the grooves on the sides. Plow these ¼-in.-deep grooves on the table saw with a ⅛-in. kerf blade and the fence set ¼ in. from the blade.

3 Cut the Plexiglas end panels to size: To avoid scratching the panels, don't remove the clear film that covers the plastic for marking or cutting. Lay out the part shapes and cut the Plexiglas to size on the band saw with a fine-toothed blade **(See Photo B)**. You can cut Plexiglas on the table saw also, but use a fine-toothed plywood-cutting blade or a blade intended to cut plastic and laminate. Otherwise, the Plexiglas will tend to chip as you cut. Gently sand the edges of each panel, then dry-fit them into the grooves in the cedar side pieces to be sure they fit. Widen the grooves if necessary on the table saw.

MAKE THE ROOF SECTIONS

4 Start by making a blank for both roof sections from one piece of stock. The board dimensions should be 6 in. wide and 10⅜ in. long. Round over both ends of the blank on the router table with a ⅜-in. roundover bit. NOTE: *Be careful when the router bit exits the board. Aromatic cedar is soft, and the end grain will tear out on the edges of the boards. Rout these bullnose profiles in several passes of increasing*

PHOTO A: Trim the gable ends of the sides on a power miter saw with the blade swiveled to 45°. Center the gable peaks across the width of the workpieces.

PHOTO B: Measure and cut the Plexiglas end panels on the band saw with a fine-toothed blade. Leave the protective film on the plastic as you machine it, to minimize scratching.

PHOTO C: Tilt the table saw blade to 45° and cut the roof blank in half to form two roof sections. Take time to set up this cut accurately. Otherwise the roof section lengths won't match. One cut both trims the parts to length and forms the roof miter joint.

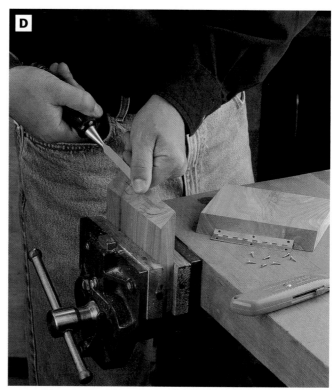

PHOTO D: Mark and cut the shallow hinge mortises into the beveled edges of the roof sections. Score along your mortise layout lines first with a utility knife, then pare out the mortise with a sharp chisel. Keep the mortise depth the same as the hinge leaf thickness.

depth, which will also help minimize chipping and tearout.

5 Split the roof blank in half to form the two roof sections. Since the roof sections meet at a 45° angle at the bird feeder peak, you'll crosscut the roof blank in half at the table saw with the blade set at a 45° bevel angle **(See Photo C)**. Be careful when setting up this cut so you'll divide the roof blank equally.

6 Cut hinge mortises into the top bevels of the roof sections: The roof halves will be joined together with a single brass jewelry box hinge. In order to form a relatively tight miter joint at the bird feeder peak, you'll need to recess the hinge leaves into shallow mortises cut into the roof sections. Lay out the hinge location on each roof section by outlining the shape of the hinge leaves along the top edge of the roof bevels. Keep the knuckle of the hinge above the bevel edge, as shown in the *Side View* drawing, page 67. Clamp each roof section in a vise, and score along your mortise layout lines with a utility knife. Then pare away the material within your layout lines with a sharp chisel **(See Photo D)**. The mortises shouldn't be deeper than the hinge leaves are thick.

BUILD THE BASE

7 Make the base strips: Rip a ¾-in.-wide stick of cedar to 16⅛ in. long on the table saw. Crosscut the workpiece in half to form two 8-in.-long base strips. Round over the ends of the strips with a wood rasp and random-orbit sander or on a stationary disk sander. NOTE: *These ends are too narrow to round over with a router without tearing out the wood.*

8 Drill holes through the ends of the base strips for the perches: Lay out the centerpoints for these perch holes on one base strip, ⅜ in. in from each end. Stack the marked base strip on top of the other strip, and clamp them to your drill press table. Use a backer board beneath the base strips to keep from drilling into the drill press table. Chuck a ¼-in.-dia. bit in the drill press, and drill holes completely through both base strips **(See Photo E)**. Dry-fit the perch doweling into the base strip holes to be sure it will fit.

9 Make the remaining base parts: Rip and crosscut the base plate to size. Measure and cut the perch dowels to length at this time as well.

10 Assemble the base. Install the perches in one of the base strips, using a dab of polyurethane glue in

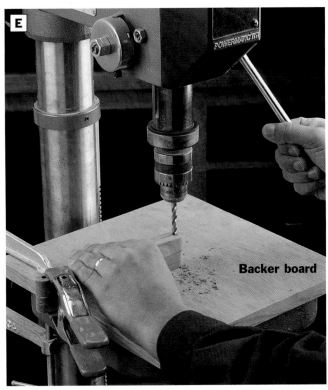

PHOTO E: Bore ¼-in.-dia. holes for the perches through both ends of the base strips. We stacked these parts and drilled both strips at once on the drill press.

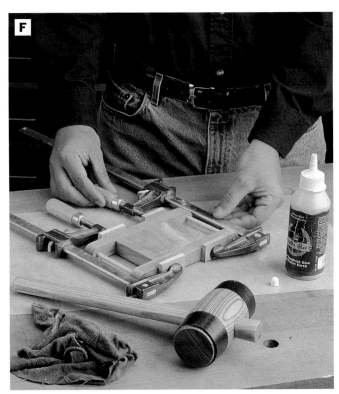

PHOTO F: Assemble the base plate, base strips and perches with polyurethane glue. Clamp the parts together to keep the glue from forcing the joints open as it cures.

each dowel hole. Apply a coat of polyurethane glue to the long edges of the base plate, and wet the mating surfaces of the base strips with a water-dampened rag. Squeeze a drop of glue into the dowel holes of the other base strip and assemble the base parts together, making sure the perches are properly seated in their holes **(See Photo F)**. Tap them gently, if needed, with a mallet. Polyurethane glue will foam and expand as it cures, so hold the base strips against the base plate with a couple of short bar clamps or large C-clamps until the glue cures. Clean up excess glue immediately with mineral spirits.

⑪ Make the feed dams: Since these parts are small, and one long edge of each receives a bullnosed profile, start from a piece of wide stock (6 in. wide or wider) and rout the bullnoses first before ripping and cross-cutting the dams to size. Routing wider stock will keep your hands a safe distance from the router bit. Round over one long edge of the workpiece on the router table with a ⅜-in.-dia. roundover bit. Then rip and crosscut the feed dams to size.

⑫ Install the feed dams on the bird feeder base. Attach the dams to the short ends of the base plate in between the base strips with polyurethane glue.

Use a clamp to hold the dams in position until the glue cures. Again, clean up excess glue before it sets.

ASSEMBLE THE BIRD FEEDER

⑬ Install the clear end panels in the grooves in the cedar sides: Spread a thin coat of two-part epoxy into each of the grooves in the sides, keeping the adhesive about 1 in. shy of the top and bottom of each groove. (Two-part epoxy is a good adhesive for bonding Plexiglas.) Remove the protective film from the Plexiglas, and slip the two end panels into their respective grooves, aligning them so they're approximately ¾ in. up from the bottoms of the sides **(See Photo G)**.

⑭ Fasten the base to the sides: Apply a bead of polyurethane glue along the bottom edge of each side, then center the sides on the base strips. Drill counter-sunk pilot holes up through the bottom of the base strips and into the sides, and drive 1½-in. galvanized wood screws into the holes **(See Photo H)**. Then drill a few 1⁄16-in.-dia. weep holes through the base, which will help keep the feed dry.

⑮ Assemble the roof: Mark and drill pilot holes for the brass screws that will attach the hinge to the roof sections. Install the hinge.

PHOTO G: Spread two-part epoxy into the grooves in the side panels, remove the protective film from the Plexiglas end pieces, and slide the end pieces into the grooves. The end pieces should stop ¾ in. from the bottoms of the sides.

16 Fasten the roof to the side panels. Spread a bead of polyurethane glue along one gable edge of each side panel. Wet the mating surfaces of one of the roof sections and set the roof in place over the sides. Be careful to align the roof so it overhangs the sides evenly. Drive a few galvanized 4d finish nails down through the glued roof section to fasten it to the sides (**See Photo I**). It's a good idea to drill pilot holes for these nails first, to keep the nails from splitting the sides. Then countersink the nailheads with a nailset.

Feeding songbirds

The type of food you provide in the feeder will in large part determine the bird species you attract. Dark-eyed juncos, for example, love millet, especially when it falls on the ground below the feeder. Sunflower seeds are a sure bet for bluejays, chickadees, cardinals, gold and purple finches, nuthatches, the tufted titmouse and pine siskens. Downy woodpeckers and blue jays also like an occasional meal of shelled peanuts. Regardless of the type of feed you use, experts agree that the feeder must be cleaned out regularly to keep the contents from molding. If the birds should consume molded seed, it can cause aspergillosis, a fatal illness for songbirds.

PHOTO H: Attach the base to the sides with polyurethane glue and 1½-in. countersunk galvanized wood screws. Then drill a few small weep holes (smaller than the seed you'll put in the feeder) to allow any moisture to drain away, keeping the birdseed dry.

PHOTO I: Attach one half of the roof to the body of the bird feeder with polyurethane glue and galvanized 4d nails. The other roof section hinges open to allow easy access for filling and cleaning the feeder.

This project proves that some toys simply aren't for kids. With its walnut case, delicate moldings and brass hardware, this chessboard project will be the perfect complement to your cherished chess set. Our design features a pair of drawers for storing chess pieces during and after a game, and the walnut-and-maple checkered top is easier to build than you might think.

Double-drawer Chessboard

Vital Statistics: Double-drawer Chessboard

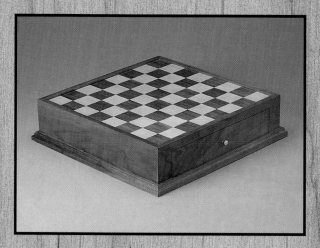

TYPE: Chessboard

OVERALL SIZE: 16W by 16D by 3¾H

MATERIAL: Walnut, maple, walnut and maple veneers

JOINERY: Dado, rabbet and butt joints

CONSTRUCTION DETAILS:

· Playing surface is composed of self-stick veneer squares on an MDF panel, to minimize wood movement
· Top and bottom pieces attach to front, back and sides with biscuits
· Drawer faces are cut from front and back pieces so the grain will match when the drawers are closed

FINISH: Satin polyurethane

Building time

 PREPARING STOCK
4 hours

 LAYOUT
3-4 hours

 CUTTING PARTS
6 hours

 ASSEMBLY
4-6 hours

 FINISHING
2 hours

TOTAL: 19-22 hours

Tools you'll use

· Table saw
· Scroll saw
· Miter saw (optional)
· Biscuit joiner
· Drill/driver
· Clamps
· Router table with ¼-in. bead bit
· J-roller (or rolling pin)

Shopping list

☐ (1) ½ × 8 in. × 6 ft. walnut
☐ (1) ½ × 4 in. × 4 ft. maple
☐ (1) ½ × 2 ft. × 4 ft. MDF
☐ (1) ¼ in. × 2 ft. × 2 ft. birch plywood
☐ (1) ¹⁄₄₀ × 2 ft. × 2 ft. walnut self-stick veneer
☐ (1) ¹⁄₄₀ × 2 ft. × 2 ft. maple self-stick veneer
☐ (2) ½-in.-dia. brass knobs
☐ (2) #6 x 1¼-in. machine screws
☐ #0 biscuits
☐ Wood glue
☐ Finishing materials

PHOTO E: Assemble the top and bottom, front, back and sides with #0 biscuits and glue to form the carcase. Protect the perimeter of the veneer top from glue squeeze-out with masking tape. Be sure the carcase is square when you clamp by measuring the diagonals. When the diagonal measurements match, the carcase is square. Adjust the clamps, if needed, to adjust for square.

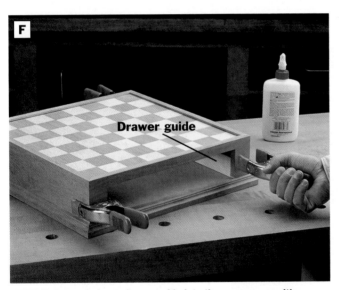

Drawer guide

PHOTO F: Cut and glue a drawer guide into the recesses on either side of the drawer openings. Clamp the guides from both sides of the chessboard while the glue dries.

9 Dry-assemble the top, bottom, sides, front and back to check the fit of the parts. Be sure the chess board grid is oriented correctly: there should be a white square on the right corner above each drawer opening. The miter joints must close tightly. If they don't, sand the edges of the top and bottom panels a little at a time to improve the fit of the miter joints.

10 Cut slots for #0 biscuits to join the carcase parts. Biscuits will make aligning the carcase parts easier during glue-up. Refer to the drawing on page 74 for locating the approximate positions of the biscuit slots. Notice that you'll cut two slots into each edge of the top and bottom pieces as well as the mating slots in the front, back and side pieces. When you cut the slots, index your biscuit joiner so that the top and bottom panels are flush with the top and bottom edges of the drawer cutouts. You may want to cut a test slot on scrap to check your joiner's depth-of-cut setting.

11 Assemble the carcase: Protect the veneered face of the top panel from glue squeeze-out by covering the perimeter with masking tape. Spread glue along the mating surfaces of the joints and into the biscuit slots, insert biscuits and clamp up the carcase. Check the assembly for square (**See Photo E**), and wipe away excess glue. Remove the masking tape after the glue stops squeezing out and before it dries.

12 Rout and install the bead molding around the base of the carcase. The safest way to mill this narrow molding is to rout the long edge of a length of ½-in.-thick stock, then trim the profiled edges off the board to form the molding. Set up your router table with a ¼-in.-radius bead bit, and rout the molding in two passes of increasing depth. Rip-cut the ¾-in.-tall moldings from the board. Miter-cut four strips to length, and attach the molding around the carcase with glue and clamps.

BUILD THE DRAWERS

13 The first step in building the drawers is to cut a pair of spacers to act as drawer guides. These are simply scrap stock, ripped to width, trimmed to length and glued into the recesses on each side of the drawer openings (**See Photo F**). Rip them about ¹⁄₁₆ in. narrower than flush so they set back slightly from the ends of the drawer openings. This will allow a bit of room for drawer play.

14 Cut the drawer fronts, backs and sides to size: Rip and crosscut these maple parts on the table saw.

15 Cut the rabbets in the drawer front and back pieces. These rabbet cuts will form a tongue on each end of the workpieces. The tongues will fit into dadoes that you'll cut in the drawer sides to form strong, interlocking joints. To make the rabbet cuts, attach a sacrificial wood fence to your table saw's rip fence, and set your dado blade to ½ in. wide. Start the saw and raise the blade so that it cuts ¼ in. into the sacrificial fence. Stop the saw and reset the fence so that ¼ of the blade protrudes beyond the fence, forming a ¼ × ¼-in. rabbet cut setup. Hold a workpiece against the miter gauge and sacrificial fence, then slide the miter gauge over the blade to cut each rabbet **(See Photo G)**. You could also cut these rabbets on the router table with a straight bit.

⑯ Cut dadoes into the drawer sides to receive the drawer front and back tongues as well as the drawer bottom. All of the dado cuts are ¼ in. wide and ¼ in. deep. Reset your dado blade and saw fence accordingly to make the tongue dadoes, then the drawer bottom dadoes.

⑰ Glue up the drawer boxes. Dry-assemble the parts to check their fit. Then spread glue onto the mating surfaces of the corner joints but not into the drawer bottom dadoes. The drawer bottoms should float freely in their grooves, without glue, to allow for wood movement. Assemble the parts and clamp the drawers.

⑱ Attach the walnut drawer faces to the drawer fronts. First, check the fit of the drawer boxes in their openings, and sand as needed until the boxes slide easily in and out. Spread glue on the drawer fronts. Set the drawer face against the drawer fronts and align each drawer face on the drawers so the bottom and ends of the drawer face are flush with the bottom and sides of the drawer boxes. Hold the drawer faces in place with spring or C-clamps until the glue dries.

FINISHING TOUCHES

⑲ Sand the entire project (except the veneered grid) with 220-grit paper. Use a tack cloth to remove any residual dust, then apply three coats of satin polyurethane varnish.

PHOTO G: Attach a sacrificial wood fence to your table saw's rip fence, and use it to establish the ¼ × ¼-in. dado blade reveal for cutting rabbets on the ends of the drawer front and back pieces. Cut the rabbets with the workpieces held against both the miter gauge and the sacrificial fence.

PHOTO H: After applying three coats of satin polyurethane, install the knobs on each drawer. Although we don't show it here, you may also want to add catches or turnbuckles for holding the drawers closed for transport.

⑳ Install the drawer knobs. Locate the centers of the drawer faces, and drill pilot holes through the faces and drawer fronts for the knob screws. Screw the knobs in place **(See Photo H)**.

DESIGN NOTE: *This chessboard was not designed to be portable or fre-quently transported. If you are likely to move yours around a lot, be sure to hold both drawers closed as you carry it in order to keep them from sliding out of their openings. Or you may want to add magnetic catches, ball catches or small turnbuckles to secure the drawers closed.*

The curved ends of this cherry container are a pleasant departure from other square-edged woodworking projects, and the project is sized generously to hold several month's worth of your favorite magazines or even books. Contemporary, clean styling makes this bin attractive as well as practical, wherever you spend time reading.

Bentwood Reader's Bin

PHOTO C: Tilt the table saw blade to 13° and bevel-cut the top and bottom ends of the stand blank. Hold the workpiece against the miter gauge to make these cuts.

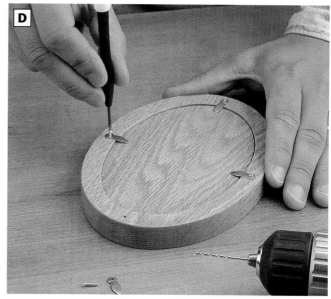

PHOTO D: Four brass turn buttons hold the glass, photo and back in the frame. Install the hardware so the turn buttons are spaced evenly around the frame. Drill pilot holes for the tiny turn button screws.

stand on your blank and cut it out on the scroll saw. Smooth the cut edges on the drum sander.

6 Make the back panel. Lay out the back on a piece of ¼-in. oak, using the *Back Layout* grid pattern on page 111 as a guide for drawing the shape. Cut out the back, and sand the edges until the back panel fits easily into the rabbet on the frame.

FINISHING TOUCHES

7 Smooth the entire project with 220-grit sandpaper. Apply several coats of clear satin polyurethane, sanding lightly between each with 320-grit paper or #0000 steel wool. Since the frame parts are small, we sprayed the varnish from an aerosol can rather than brushing on the finish.

8 Install the glass, back and turn buttons. Drill pilot holes for the tiny turn button screws (**See Photo D**).

9 Attach the hinge to the frame and stand with screws, bolts and nuts. Since the hinge is small and the space confined, install it as follows: Mark the hinge position on the frame back and on the stand as shown in the *Back Layout* drawing, page 111. Mount the hinge to the frame back first with ¼-in. flathead wood screws driven into pilot holes. Slip two #4 × ½-in. bolts through holes in the hinge leaf that will be attached to the stand, so the heads of the bolts face the frame. Drill holes through the stand for the hinge bolts. Then slide the bolts through the holes in the

PHOTO E: After locating the hinge position, mount the hinge to the frame back with #4 × ¼-in. brass flathead wood screws. Fasten the hinge to the stand with bolts and nuts. Arrange the bolts so you can thread the nuts on from the back of the stand. Tighten the nuts and bolts with a pair of needle-nose pliers.

stand and attach with nuts (**See Photo E**). Tighten the nuts with needle-nose pliers. File the bolt ends flush with the nuts.

10 Mount your photo. Remove the frame back and use it as a template for tracing a cutting line onto your photo. Trim the photo to shape, slip it into place and reinstall the frame back.

A favorite in the courts of medieval kings, the ball-&-cup game was designed to improve hand/eye coordination. Getting the small cylindrical "ball" to drop into the cup on the handle isn't as easy as it looks. But making the game is fairly simple; despite its cylindrical shape, you won't even need a lathe. The handle and cup are shaped entirely on a drill press.

Ball-&-Cup Game

Vital Statistics: Ball-&-Cup Game

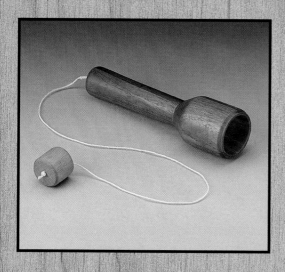

TYPE: Ball-&-cup game

OVERALL SIZE: 1½ Dia. by 6L

MATERIAL: Walnut, hardwood dowel

JOINERY: Face-glued butt joints (handle blank)

CONSTRUCTION DETAILS:
- Handle is turned on a drill press and shaped with rasps and files
- Hole bored into the cup end of the handle on the drill press with the table tipped vertically
- Cylindrical "ball" made from a length of dowel with chamfered edges

FINISH: Paste wax or shellac

Building time

PREPARING STOCK
1-2 hours

LAYOUT
1 hour

SHAPING PARTS
1-2 hours

ASSEMBLY
½ hour

FINISHING
½ hour

TOTAL: 4-6 hours

Tools you'll use

- Table saw
- Band saw or jig saw
- Belt sander
- Compass
- Hand plane
- Drill press with 1¼-in. Forstner bit
- Rasps
- Files

Shopping list

- ☐ (1) ¾ × 2 in. by 2 ft. or 2 × 2 × 6½-in. walnut
- ☐ (1) 1-in.-dia. dowel
- ☐ ¼ × 2-in. bolt
- ☐ 4d finish nail
- ☐ ⅝-in. screw eye
- ☐ Kite string
- ☐ Wood glue
- ☐ Finishing materials

Ball-&-Cup Game

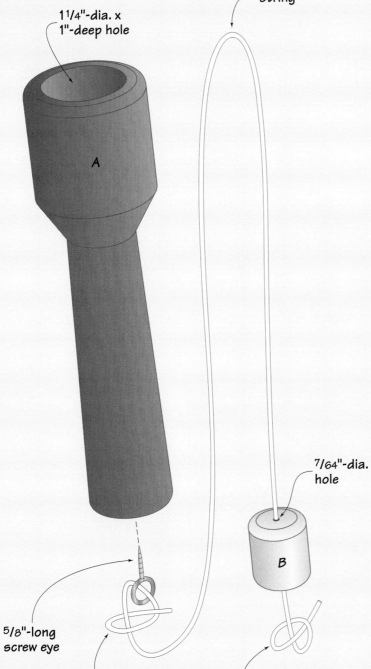

1¼"-dia. x 1"-deep hole

20"-long string

7/64"-dia. hole

A

B

5/8"-long screw eye

double half hitch knot

stopper knot

Grid squares are 1" x 1"

1¼"

1¼"

A

₵

CUP & HANDLE LAYOUT

Ball-&-Cup Game Cutting List			
Part	**No.**	**Size**	**Material**
A. Handle	1	2 × 2 × 6½ in.	Walnut
B. Ball	1	1-in.-dia. × ⅞ in.	Dowel

PREPARE A HANDLE BLANK

1 If you are building the handle from ¾-in. stock, crosscut three 2-in.-wide pieces to 6½ in. long. Face-glue and clamp the pieces together. Rip-cut the blank so it's 2 in. square. Otherwise, rip and crosscut a solid piece of thick walnut to size.

2 Rough the handle blank into a cylinder. First, find the center-points on the ends of the blank by drawing diagonal lines from corner to corner on both ends. The intersection of the lines marks the centerpoints. Draw a 1½-in.-dia. circle around these centerpoints with a compass. Then clamp the blank in a vise or against a bench dog, knock off the four long cor-ners with a belt sander and shave away the remaining waste down to your circular layout lines with a sharp hand plane to form a rough cylinder (**See Photo A**).

MOUNT THE HANDLE BLANK ON A DRILL PRESS

Your drill press wasn't designed to be a lathe, but it still can be converted into an effective shap-ing tool. Here are a couple things to keep in mind: You'll be shaping the handle working vertically instead of horizontally. You'll also be working without a tool rest. For these reasons, you won't use bladed tools for making this turn-

PHOTO A: It's best to turn the handle from a cylindrical blank. Knock off the long, square corners of the blank, then shave off the remaining waste down to your circular layout lines marked on the ends of the blank with a hand plane. Plane lengthwise, with the grain.

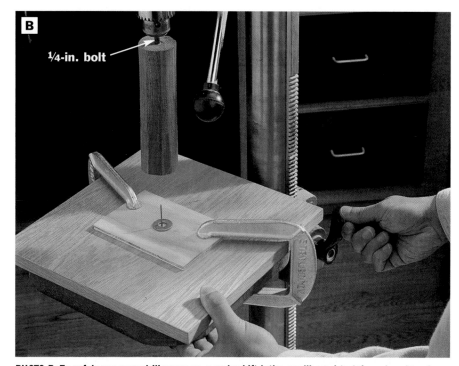

PHOTO B: To safely use your drill press as a makeshift lathe, you'll need to take extra steps to ensure that the workpiece is held securely. A ¼-in. bolt screwed into the top of the blank holds the workpiece in the drill press chuck, while a finish nail driven through a piece of plywood and clamped to the drill press table forms a "dead center" for the bottom end of the blank.

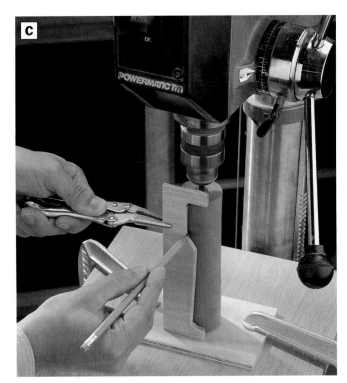

PHOTO C: With the drill press turning at low speed, mark the blank where the handle profiles change—at the bottom of the cup, the top of the handle and the bottom of the handle. Hold the pencil lightly against the template and the blank to mark the reference lines.

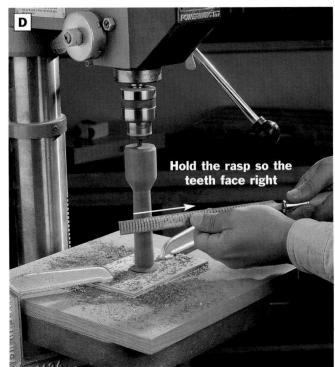

Hold the rasp so the teeth face right

PHOTO D: Drag a rasp against the spinning blank to begin removing waste. Use your reference lines to define the shape of the handle, and stop occasionally to verify your progress against the profile template.

ing. Rasps and files are a safer alternative for accomplishing the shaping work.

3 Set up the drill press: Drive a 4d finish nail up through the center of a piece of ¼-in. plywood about 6 to 8 in. square. Lay the plywood on the drill press table, then raise the table until about half the nail is inside the chuck. Close the chuck on the nail (this will center the nail under the chuck), then secure the plywood to the table with a couple of C-clamps. Open the chuck to release the nail, and lower the table about 8 in. straight down. Place a large metal washer over the nail to serve as a spacer between the handle and the plywood. The nail is now the bottom axis (or "dead center") on which the handle blank will spin.

4 Install the handle blank in the drill press: Drill a ¹⁄₁₆-in.-dia. hole 1 in. deep into the center of one end of the handle blank and a ⁷⁄₃₂-in.-dia. hole 1 in. into the other end. Twist the ¼-in. bolt all the way into the larger hole. Saw off the bolt head with a hack saw. Tighten the bolt stub into the drill press chuck and raise the table so the nail enters the bottom hole in the blank **(See Photo B)**. Set the table height so the bottom of the handle blank rests on the washer to complete the "lathe" setup.

Turn the handle shape

5 Make a template for the handle: Lay out a full-size template for the handle profile on a piece of scrap plywood or hardboard (See *Cup & Handle Layout* drawing, page 116). Cut out the template. You'll use the template to mark the handle blank and check your progress as you rough it into shape.

6 Mark reference lines on the blank: Set your drill press speed to 500 rpm and turn on the machine. Lay the profile template next to the spinning blank and touch a pencil to the blank to mark the bottom of the cup, top of the handle and bottom of the handle. This will produce pencil lines around the blank at each reference point **(See Photo C)**.

7 Rough out the handle profile: Hold a coarse rasp firmly in both hands so the cutting teeth face your right hand (which will be against the rotation of the drill press). Press the rasp flat against the front of the spinning blank to begin grinding off the waste. Continue to work the rasp against the workpiece until you've formed the handle profile **(See Photo D)**. Check your progress every so often by stopping the drill press and laying the template against the workpiece. When the handle shape closely matches the template, change to a file for finishing the shape.

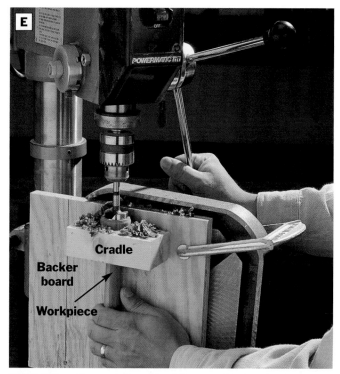

PHOTO E: Bore the cup hole on the drill press with the table in a vertical position (tilted 90°). Hold the handle workpiece in place by sliding it into a 1½-in.-dia. hole on a scrap cradle mounted to a backer board that is clamped to the table. Drill the 1¼-in.-dia. cup hole 1 in. deep.

8 Switch to sandpaper to smooth the handle. Start with 60-grit, holding the ends of the paper so the middle rubs against and conforms to the handle shape as it spins. Work all the way up to 400-grit with progressively smoother papers. Finish with steel wool to produce a fine, polished surface. When you reach the level of smoothness that suits you, hold a cloth loaded with paste wax or shellac against the spinning handle to rub on the finish. Then burnish the finish with a dry cloth.

9 Remove the handle from the drill press and trim off the bottom waste on the band saw. Wipe finish onto the handle bottom.

BORE THE CUP HOLE

10 Drill the 1¼-in.-dia. hole in the top of the handle to form the cup. This is easiest to do if you tip the drill press table to vertical and clamp the handle to the table. TIP: *We bored a 1½-in.-dia. hole through a thick piece of scrap to form a cradle, screwed it to a backer board and clamped the board to the drill press table. To drill the cup hole, slide the handle into the hole in the scrap and align the handle under the drill bit* (**See Photo E**). Drill the cup hole 1 in. deep.

11 Sand the cup hole, and wipe on a coat of finish.

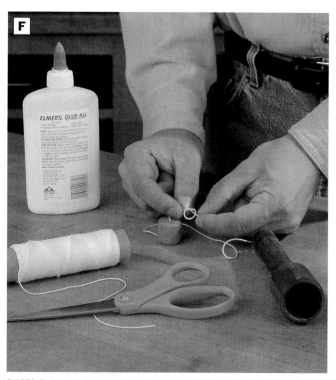

PHOTO F: Attach the ball and handle together with a length of kite string. Tie the string to the screw eye on the handle, thread the other end through the hole in the ball, and knot securely. A drop of glue on each knot will keep it from loosening or fraying.

ADD THE STRING & BALL

12 Thread a ⅝-in. screw eye into the nail hole in the bottom of the handle.

13 Make the "ball." Cut a ⅞-in. length of 1-in.-dia. dowel, then sand a chamfer around the top and bottom edges. Locate the center of the ball and drill a ⁷⁄₆₄-in.-dia. hole all the way through it for the string. Cover it with a coat of finish.

14 Connect the ball to the screw eye with a 20-in. length of kite string, then thread the string through the hole in the ball and knot it several times (**See Photo F**). Cover each knot with a drop of white glue to hold the knots securely and to keep the ends of the string from fraying.

Here's the secret to this game:

The best way to make the ball fall into the cup is to have it hang perfectly still, directly below the handle, then quickly jerk the handle upward so the ball goes straight up. Move the cup under the ball quickly so it drops into place.

If you play table tennis, why not table hockey? This game will be a sure hit with parents because it is one of those rare toys these days that doesn't require batteries. Build our version of the game from ash and melamine hardboard in a single day. No waiting for ice time here!

Table Hockey

Vital Statistics: Table Hockey

TYPE: Hockey game table

OVERALL SIZE: 18½W by 4H by 48L

MATERIAL: Ash, white melamine hardboard

JOINERY: Tongue-and-dado, butt-and-rabbet joints

CONSTRUCTION DETAILS:
· Box corners reinforced with rabbet joints
· Tongue-and-dado joints fasten goals to sides
· Parts finished prior to assembly to make finish application easy

FINISH: Ash parts finished with two coats of gloss polyurethane varnish

Building time

PREPARING STOCK
1 hour

LAYOUT
2-3 hours

CUTTING PARTS
3-4 hours

ASSEMBLY
1-2 hours

FINISHING
1 hour

TOTAL: 8-11 hours

Tools you'll use

· Table saw
· Dado blade
· Band saw or jig saw
· Drill/driver
· Power miter saw (optional)
· Router with ¼-in. straight bit
· Clamps

Shopping list

☐ (2) 4/4 × 9 in. × 10 ft. ash

☐ (1) ¼ in. × 2 ft. × 4 ft. white melamine hardboard

☐ #8 flathead wood screws (1-, 1½-in.)

☐ Wood glue

☐ Finishing materials

BUILD THE SIDES & ENDS

1 Make the sides and ends: Surface-plane your 4/4 ash stock to ¾ in. thick. Rip and crosscut the two sides and ends to size. Then mill grooves in all four workpieces to house the playing surface. To do this, install a ¼-in. straight bit in your router table. Set the bit height to ¼ in. and the router fence ½ in. from the bit. Mill a groove along one edge of each side and end that runs the full length of the workpieces **(See Photo A)**. You could also make these grooves with a table saw and dado blade.

2 Mill stopped grooves in the sides for the goals: Clamp a straightedge on each side piece so you can rout a ¼-in.-wide groove 3¼ in. from each end of both sides (See *Top View Sides,* page 123). Rout these grooves ¼ in. deep, and stop the cuts when the bit intersects the playing surface grooves **(See Photo B)**. Rout all four of these short grooves.

3 Cut rabbets on both ends of the end pieces. Set up your table saw and dado blade to cut these ¾-in.-wide, ½-in.-deep rabbets. Cut the rabbets on the same side of each workpiece as the groove for the playing surface. You could cut these rabbets on your router table as well, with a ¾-in. straight bit.

4 Cut the angled profiles on the end pieces: Lay out the end profiles using the *Front & Top View Ends* drawing, page 123, as a guide. Make these cuts on the band saw or with a jig saw.

MAKE THE CENTERBOARD, GOALS & PLAYING SURFACE

5 Mark and cut the centerboard: Rip and crosscut a blank for the centerboard. See the *Front View Centerboard* drawing, page 123, to lay out the concave arch along the top edge as well as the two square notches on the bottom ends. Trim the arch and notches on the

PHOTO A: Rout a ¼ × ¼-in. groove in the end and side pieces to house the playing surface. These dadoes are located ½ in. from the edges of the parts and run the full length.

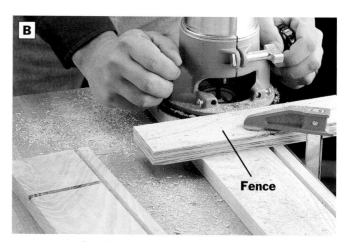

PHOTO B: Rout ¼ × ¼-in. dadoes in the side pieces for the goals. Clamp a fence to the workpiece to ensure straight cuts. Stop these dado cuts where they intersect the grooves for the playing surface.

PHOTO C: Band-saw the notched bottom ends and the arch along the top edge of the centerboard.

band saw (**See Photo C**). Sand the edges smooth.

❻ Make the two goals: Rip and crosscut workpieces for the goals. Then set up your table saw and dado blade or router table and straight bit to cut ¼ × ¼-in. centered tenons on the ends of the goals. The tenons run the full 3¼-in. width of the goals. Then measure, mark and cut the 1½-in.-tall, 2-in.-wide rectangular goal cutout along the bottom edge of both workpieces. The goal cutout is centered along the length of the parts.

❼ Cut the hardboard playing surface to size. Draw a heavy blue line 13³⁄₁₆ in. from each end across the board's width with a permanent marker and straightedge. Make the blue lines ¼ in. thick.

APPLY A FINISH & ASSEMBLE

❽ Dry-fit all the game parts together, then disassemble and sand the ash pieces thoroughly. Mask the rabbets and tenon areas to protect them from finish, then apply two coats of gloss polyurethane to all the ash parts (**See Photo D**). Sand between coats of finish with 320-grit wet/dry paper or #0000 steel wool. Remove the masking tape.

❾ Build the box: Spread glue along the rabbets on the end pieces, and assemble the sides, playing surface and ends. (The playing surface requires no glue in its grooves.) Clamp the box and measure the diagonals to be sure it's square. Then spread glue on the tenon ends of the goals, and slide the goals into place in their grooves.

❿ Install the centerboard: Mark centerpoints along the length of the sides. Set the centerboard between the sides and align it with

PHOTO D: Durable gloss polyurethane is a good finish choice for a project like this that is bound to get hard use. Mask off the tongue and rabbet joints first, to keep them free of varnish.

PHOTO E: Attach the centerboard with countersunk wood screws driven through the side pieces, one screw per side. Drive two screws up from below and into the bottom of the centerboard.

the marks you just drew. Drill a countersunk pilot hole through each side and into the centerboard ends, and fasten the parts together with #8 × 1½-in. flathead wood screws (**See Photo E**). Then drive three more 1-in. screws up through the playing surface along

the length of the centerboard bottom to stiffen the playing surface.

⓫ Fashion playing sticks from short pieces of leftover ash, or use popsicle sticks instead. Plastic checker pieces make good pucks.

Rules of play

Part of the fun of playing box hockey is that players make up the rules. Here are some general guidelines: At face-off, the younger player serves the puck from the top of the centerboard, aiming at the opponent's goal. Then, players alternate shooting the puck through the centerboard notches and onto their opponent's "ice," where they have an agreed-upon number of shots to attempt a goal. Opponents do not guard the goal. Blue-line rules can be made any way players see fit. The first player to score 11 goals wins. The winner must win by two goals.

Library Bookends

These sturdy white-oak bookends will support reading materials of all sizes—including oversized books. To help keep the bookends stationary, you can drill holes in the bases and fill them with metal ballast. A layer of walnut, sandwiched between the vertical oak frames, adds a sophisticated touch.

Vital Statistics: Library Bookends

TYPE: Bookends

OVERALL SIZE: 8½W by 11¾H by 8L

MATERIAL: White oak, walnut

JOINERY: Butt joints reinforced with glue and screws

CONSTRUCTION DETAILS:

· Holes in the bases are filled with ballast and hidden by base caps

· All exposed edges are rounded over with the router

· Cutout edges on frames receive routed chamfers

FINISH: Satin polyurethane varnish

Building time

PREPARING STOCK
1 hour

LAYOUT
1 hour

CUTTING PARTS
2-3 hours

ASSEMBLY
3-4 hours

FINISHING
1 hour

TOTAL: 8-10 hours

Tools you'll use

· Table saw
· Scroll saw
· Drill/driver
· Router with ¼-in. roundover bit, 45° piloted chamfering bit
· Drill press with 1¼-in. Forstner bit
· Jointer (optional)
· Planer
· Files
· Clamps

Shopping list

☐ (1) ¾ × 10 in. × 6 ft. white oak

☐ (1) ¾ × 6 in. × 8 ft. white oak

☐ (1) ¾ × 8 in. × 2 ft. walnut

☐ #8 flathead wood screws (1½-, 2-in.)

☐ Ballast (steel shot, sinkers, small nails, bolts, etc.)

☐ Wood glue

☐ Finishing materials

START WITH THE BASES

1 Laminate the bases together: First, rip and cross-cut the four base pieces to size, according to the *Cutting List* dimensions on page 128. Glue pairs of base pieces together to form two 1½-in.-thick bases.

2 Round over the top edges of each base assembly: Ease one end and two edges around the top face of each base assembly with a router and ¼-in. roundover bit.

3 Bore the ballast holes in the bases (optional). Lay out the locations of the ballast holes on the bases, following the *Bases* drawing on page 129. Drill the 12 holes in each base with a 1¼-in. Forstner bit on the drill press **(See Photo A)**.

ASSEMBLE THE FRAMES & DIVIDERS

4 Cut the eight frame pieces to size and shape: First, crosscut eight 7⅛-in.-long blanks from your 6-in.-wide white oak board. Lay out the frame shape (See the *Frames & Divider* drawing, page 129) onto one of the blanks, and cut out the frame piece. Remove the center cutout area by drilling relief holes at each of the cutout corners large enough for a scroll saw blade, then trim out the waste piece on the scroll saw. Clean up the cut edges with a file and sandpaper. Use this frame piece as a pattern for tracing the shape on the other seven workpieces. Cut them all to shape **(See Photo B)**.

5 Join the frames together and ease the edges: Glue and clamp pairs of frames together to form four frame assemblies. Be sure the edges and ends of the parts are flush. When the glue dries, rout around the cutout area on one face of each frame assembly with a piloted 45° chamfer bit set to a depth of ³⁄₁₆ in. Then ease the top end and angled and back edges of this chamfered face with a router and ¼-in. roundover bit.

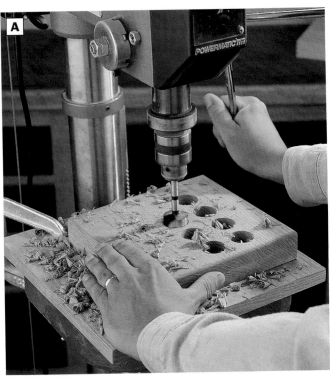

PHOTO A: *(Optional)* Drill three rows of 1¼-in.-dia. holes into the top face of both bases with a Forstner bit in the drill press. These holes will be filled with ballast and concealed by the base caps.

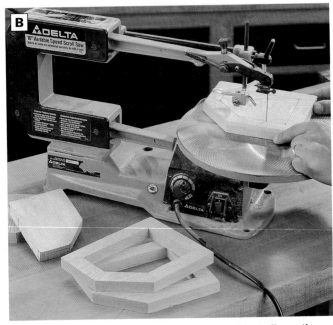

PHOTO B: Lay out and cut one frame to shape on the scroll saw, then use this first frame piece as a pattern for tracing the shapes of the other seven frames. To remove the center cutout from each frame, drill relief holes at each corner of the cutout so you can turn the workpiece on the scroll saw as you cut.

6 Make the dividers: Rip and crosscut blanks for the walnut dividers. Transfer the shape of the divider onto one of the blanks, following the *Frames & Divider* drawing on page 129. Cut the divider to shape, trace its profile onto the second walnut blank and cut out the other divider. Rout the top ends and angled and back edges with the ¼-in. roundover bit.

7 Glue up the frames and dividers: Spread glue over the inside faces of two frame assemblies and sandwich them around a divider. Clamp up the parts, making sure the flat, square edges of the three parts are flush. Then flatten the flush edges and ends of both frame/divider assemblies on a jointer (**See Photo C**). You could also use a stationary sander.

MAKE THE BASE CAPS & FRONT PLATES

8 Cut the two base caps to size, then round over one end and two edges of the top face of each cap with a router and ¼-in. roundover bit.

9 Make the front plates. Surface-plane an 8-in.-wide, 20⅝-in. oak blank down to ⅝ in. thick. Crosscut the blank in half to form the two front plates, and sand the parts smooth.

ASSEMBLE THE BOOKENDS

10 Fasten the base caps to the frame/dividers. Glue and screw a base cap to each frame/divider, so the flat end (without the roundover) of the base cap is flush with the long, flat edge of the frame/divider. Drive four countersunk 1¼-in. wood screws up through the base caps to attach them to the frame/dividers. See the *Base Cap* drawing, page 129, for screw placement.

11 Install the bases. First, fill the ballast holes with weight (steel shot, sinkers, brads or short screws will all do the trick). Then glue and screw the bases to the base caps with four countersunk 2-in. flathead wood screws (**See Photo D**). Note that the flat end of each base cap assembly is set back ⅝ in. from the flat end (without the roundover) of the bases to leave room for installing the front plate.

12 Fasten the front plates to the bookends with four countersunk 1¼-in. flathead wood screws and glue (**See Photo E**).

FINISHING TOUCHES

13 Break any remaining sharp edges with sandpaper and clean up residual glue squeeze-out. Apply three coats of clear polyurethane varnish.

PHOTO C: Flatten the long edges and bottom ends of the frame/divider assemblies on the jointer or sander. The purpose here is to produce flat, even surfaces to attach to the base caps and front plates.

PHOTO D: Attach the bases to the frame/base cap subassemblies with glue and countersunk 2-in. wood screws. Clamp and fasten the parts together carefully to keep from spilling the ballast.

PHOTO E: Position the front plates on top of the bases, clamp them in place and attach them to the frame/divider assemblies with glue and four 1¼-in. flathead wood screws.

Dial-A-Bird

Although you can't pick your family, you can choose your feathered friends with this unique bird house. A fellow woodworker designed this clever plan and passed it on to us. This bird house has a rotating dial with four holes of varying diameters drilled through it. The entrance hole you choose influences which species of birds are likely to take up residence. Build one for every bird lover on your gift list.

Vital Statistics: Dial-A-Bird

TYPE: Bird house

OVERALL SIZE: 7⅜W by 8⅛H by 10L

MATERIAL: Cedar

JOINERY: Rabbet, butt joints

CONSTRUCTION DETAILS:

· Sides fitted with rabbets on both ends to fit the front and back
· Sides cut ⅜ in. short of roof members to provide for ventilation
· A bead of polyurethane glue along roof peak seals out leaks

FINISH: None

Building time

PREPARING STOCK
1 hour

LAYOUT
1-2 hours

CUTTING PARTS
1-2 hours

ASSEMBLY
2-3 hours

FINISHING
None

TOTAL: 5-8 hours

Tools you'll use

· Planer
· Table saw
· Dado blade (optional)
· Band saw
· Clamps
· Router table with ½-in. straight bit (optional)
· Drill press or drill/driver with 1⅛-, 1¼-, 1⅜- and 1½-in. Forstner or spade bits

Shopping list

☐ (1) ¾ × 6 in. × 6 ft. cedar
☐ 4d galvanized finish nails
☐ (4) #8 × 1¼-in. galvanized deck screws
☐ (1) #8 × ⅞-in. stainless-steel screw
☐ Polyurethane glue

PREPARE THE STOCK

❶ Choose a cedar board that is knot-free and straight, and plane it down to ½ in. thick. If you don't have access to a power planer, resaw the board on your band saw (See page 7). You can also resaw on the table saw. To do this, stand the board on edge and rip-cut both long edges with the blade raised to about 1½ in. Make additional rip cuts, raising the blade 1 in. with each pair of passes, until the final pass slices the board in two.

BUILD THE FRONT, BACK, SIDES & BASE

❷ Cut two 6⅞-in.-long blanks for the front and back. The front and back are the same shape and size, so you can lay out and cut both parts at once. Refer to the *Detail: Front & Back* drawing, page 135, to lay out the shape on one of these blanks. Stack the parts and cut both to shape on the band saw **(See Photo A)**. Stay just outside your layout lines as you cut, and sand the sawn edges up to your layout lines. Then drill the 1½-in.-dia. hole through the front piece.

❸ Make the sides: Rip and cross-cut the sides to size according to the *Cutting List,* page 134. Notice on the *Top View Sides* drawing, page 135, that the front and back fit into rabbets in the sides. Cut these ¼-in.-deep, ½-in.-wide

rabbets with a router table and straight bit or on the table saw with a dado blade.

❹ Rip and crosscut the base to size. Then trim ¾ in. of material off the front corners of your base at 45° angles, and ease the sharp edges with sandpaper.

ASSEMBLE THE PARTS

❺ Attach the sides to the front and back: Spread polyurethane glue into the side rabbets, wet the mating edges of the front and back pieces with water, and set the parts together. Stretch strips of masking tape across the joints to hold the parts in place, then drive 4d galvanized finish nails through pilot holes in the sides to attach the parts. Set the nailheads below the surface **(See Photo B)**.

❻ Install the base: Drill counter-sunk pilot holes through the base and up into the front and back pieces. Fasten the parts with 1¼-in. galvanized deck screws, two screws into the front and two into the back. Don't glue the base in place—you'll need to remove it from time to time for cleaning.

MAKE & INSTALL THE ROOF

❼ Rip and crosscut the roof segments to size. Then tilt your table saw blade to 45° and bevel-cut one long edge of each segment. The beveled edges will form a miter joint at the roof peak.

❽ Install the roof segments: Align the roof pieces so they are flush with the back of the house. Use polyurethane glue and 4d nails to attach the roof segments, setting

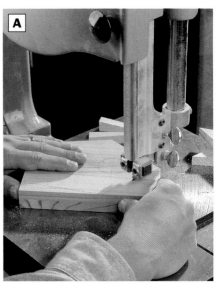

PHOTO A: Lay out and cut the front and back to shape. Since the parts are identically sized, gang-cut them on the band saw.

Recommended entry hole diameters by species

The four holes in the dial are sized to fit the following bird species:

1⅛-in. hole
- *Chickadee*
- *Prothonotary Warbler*

1¼-in. hole
- *Titmouse*
- *Red-breasted Nuthatch*
- *Downy Woodpecker*
- *House Wren*

1⅜-in. hole
- *White-breasted Nuthatch*
- *Tree & Violet-Gree Swallows*

1½-in. hole
- *Eastern & Western Bluebird*
- *Mountain Bluebird*
- *Ash-throated Flycatcher*
- *Hairy Woodpecker*
- *Yellow-bellied Sapsucker*

PHOTO B: Attach the sides to the front and back with polyurethane glue and finish nails. Use strips of masking tape to hold the parts together while you drive and set the nails.

PHOTO C: Attach the roof halves to the house with polyurethane glue and galvanized finish nails. The roof is flush to the house back. Be sure to run a generous bead of glue along the peak to seal out leaks.

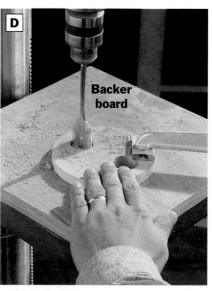

PHOTO D: Carefully lay out the hole locations on the dial, then use either spade bits or Forstner bits in the drill press to bore the four holes. Attach a backer board to the drill press table to minimize tearout on the dial.

the nailheads below the surface of the wood (**See Photo C**). The glue joint at the roof peak will seal the roof against leaks.

BUILD THE DIAL

9 Cut out the dial and drill the access holes: Mark and cut the 5-in.-dia. dial on the band saw. Refer to the *Detail: Dial* drawing, page 135, to lay out the dial hole locations. It's important that the holes are located correctly, or they won't line up with the hole in the front of the birdhouse when the dial is installed. Drill the holes with Forstner or spade bits, using a scrap backer board on the drill press table (**See Photo D**) to avoid excessive tearout.

10 Attach the dial to the birdhouse with a ⅞-in. stainless-steel wood screw (**See Photo E**).

MOUNTING TIPS

Mount the birdhouse at least 6 ft. above the ground on a post, from a tree limb or attached to a wall. Unscrew the base after each season for cleaning.

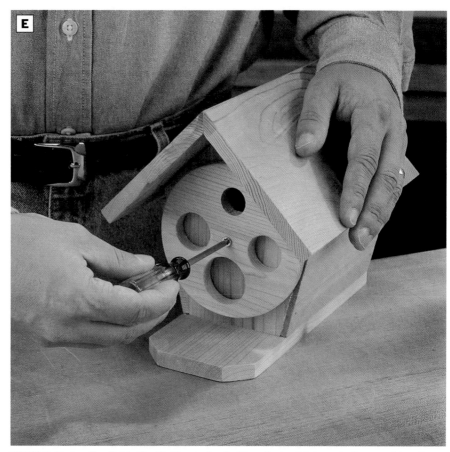

PHOTO E: Fasten the dial to the bird house front with a single stainless-steel screw, driven into a countersunk pilot hole. Drill a pilot hole in the dial large enough to allow the dial to pivot on the screw, yet small enough to hold the screw securely in the front panel.

Band Saw Box

This heart-shaped box with swiveling lid is the perfect size for storing small trinkets or jewelry. It's simple to construct and provides a great opportunity to practice your band-sawing skills, but you need to follow the sequence of cutting steps carefully—you'll build the box from only one thick block of laminated maple boards. Once you understand the series of steps required to cut out this box, follow the same cutting process to design other boxes in whatever shapes you like.

Vital Statistics: Band Saw Box

TYPE: Band saw box

OVERALL SIZE: 5W by 2¾H by 5½L

MATERIAL: Maple

JOINERY: Face-glued butt joints

CONSTRUCTION DETAILS:

- Box made of a single piece of maple, cut and laminated together to form a thick blank
- Box height is limited by your band saw's throat dimensions and the highest setting of the guard that shields the blade
- Expect to do considerable sanding when building this box out of maple. A drill press drum sander or spindle sander will make the task faster and easier

FINISH: Satin polyurethane varnish

Building time

 PREPARING STOCK
1 hour

 LAYOUT
1 hour

 CUTTING PARTS
1 hour

 ASSEMBLY
1 hour

 FINISHING
1 hour

TOTAL: 5 hours

Tools you'll use

- Band saw
- Drill press
- Drum-sanding attachment or spindle sander
- Belt sander
- Router with ³⁄₁₆-in. roundover bit
- Marking gauge
- File

Shopping list

- ☐ (1) ⁴⁄₄ × 6 in. × 2 ft. maple
- ☐ (1) ³⁄₈ × 2½-in. hardwood toy wheel axle (used as hinge pin)
- ☐ Wood glue
- ☐ Finishing materials

Band Saw Box

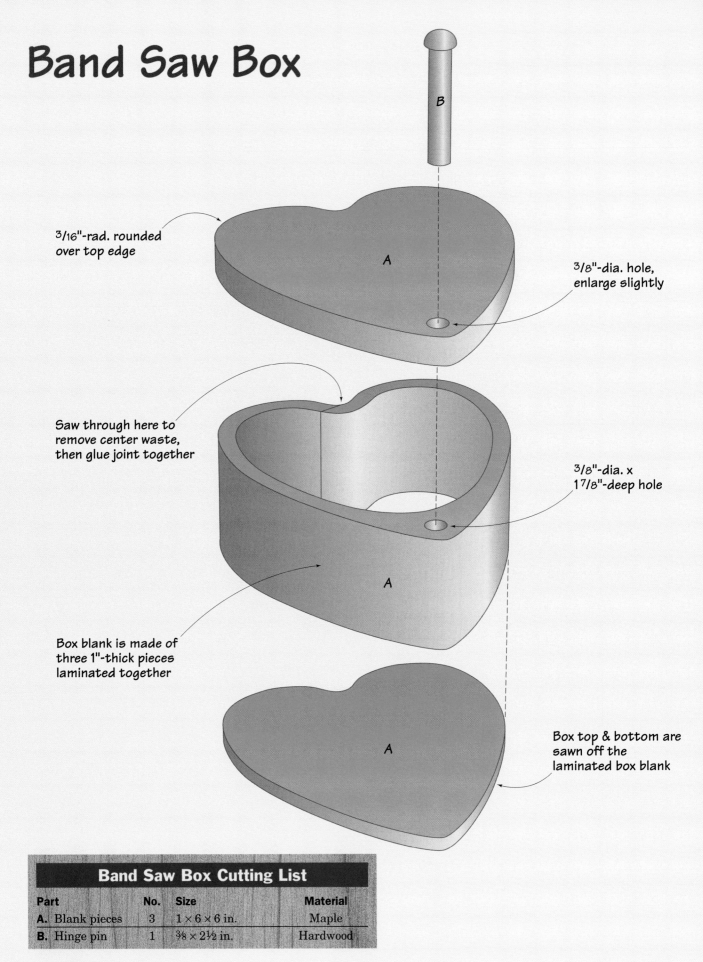

3/16"-rad. rounded over top edge

3/8"-dia. hole, enlarge slightly

Saw through here to remove center waste, then glue joint together

3/8"-dia. x 1 7/8"-deep hole

Box blank is made of three 1"-thick pieces laminated together

Box top & bottom are sawn off the laminated box blank

Band Saw Box Cutting List			
Part	**No.**	**Size**	**Material**
A. Blank pieces	3	1 × 6 × 6 in.	Maple
B. Hinge pin	1	3/8 × 2 1/2 in.	Hardwood

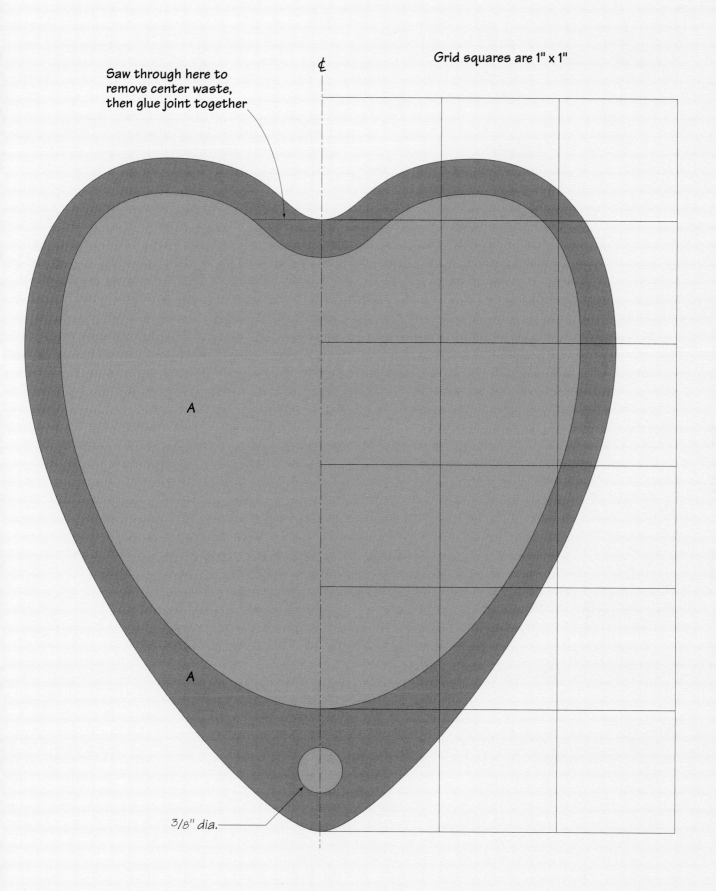

Saw through here to remove center waste, then glue joint together

Grid squares are 1" x 1"

A

A

3/8" dia.

BOX TOP, CENTER & BOTTOM LAYOUT

GLUE UP THE BLANK

The secret to band saw boxes is that they are cut entirely from one block of stock (either a glued-up blank or a single piece of wood), and the saw kerfs are glued together in such a way that they nearly disappear. It's important to carefully follow the sequence of cuts for making the box; otherwise you could inadvertently cut through the box lid or bottom instead of cutting these parts off the bigger blank, first.

1 Build the maple blank: Surface-plane both faces of the 4/4 maple stock until it is flat and smooth. Flatten one long edge of the board on a jointer. Then crosscut the six blank laminations to length. Make these cuts on the table saw or power miter saw with the flat edge of the board held against the fence of a power miter saw or against the miter gauge on a table saw. Finally, spread wood glue over both faces of one of the three laminations, and sandwich it between the other two. Clamp up the blank until the joints between the boards close tightly.

CUT OUT THE HEART

2 Enlarge the grid pattern shown on page 141 to full size, and use it to draw the inside and outside profiles of the heart on the maple blank.

3 Cut the heart's outside profile from the blank: Install a sharp 3/16-in.-wide or narrower blade in your band saw—you'll need to use a narrow blade in order to negotiate the tight curved portions of the heart. Cut just outside the outer layout line—you'll sand up to the line in order to remove saw marks and burns left by the band saw **(See Photo A)**.

4 Sand the cut edges. Use a spindle sander or a drum sander chucked in the drill press. For severe burns, start with coarse, 80-grit sandpaper and work your way down to 220-grit. Sand until you remove all

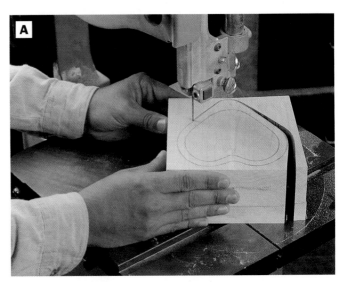

PHOTO A: Transfer the heart pattern onto the maple blank, then cut out the outside heart profile on the band saw. Use a narrow blade to make cutting the tight curves easier.

PHOTO B: With the box cut to shape, and before any of the interior cuts are made, choose one face of the blank that will become the lid. Round over the edges of this face with a 3/16-in. piloted roundover bit. Set the box on a non-slip pad to hold the workpiece securely as you rout.

blade and burn marks. While you are at it, sand the top and bottom of the blank with a belt or pad sander to the same final grit.

5 Ease the edges around the box lid: Choose the most attractive face of the blank for the lid of the box, then round over the edges with a router and 3/16-in. piloted roundover bit **(See Photo B)**.

PHOTO C: Starting at the hollow at the top of the heart, cut through the box wall and follow the inside cutting line to remove the inner waste of the heart. Do not make this cut until you've cut off the bottom and lid.

6 Cut off the box lid and bottom: Using a marking gauge, draw around the sides of the box to mark cutting lines for the ⅜-in.-thick box lid and ¼-in.-thick box bottom. Be sure your band saw table is set exactly perpendicular to the blade to keep the thickness of the top and bottom consistent as you cut. Make the cuts slowly, and hold the box in the same relationship to the blade throughout the cuts.

REMOVE THE INSIDE WASTE

7 Cut away the waste from inside the heart (**See Photo C**). Use your full-size pattern again and mark the location of the inside wall on the blank. Note that the cut will begin in the hollow at the top of the heart. This is the spot where the glued-up kerf will be least noticeable. Once the cut is complete, glue the kerf back together, using masking tape to hold the joint closed. Then drum-sand the inside of the box thoroughly.

8 Reattach the box bottom to the heart: Glue the bottom in place, then sand the edges of the bottom until they fit flush with the box sides and all traces of glue squeeze-out are removed (**See Photo D**).

9 Drill a hole in the box for the hinge pin. Use the drawing on page 141 to locate the ⅜-in.-dia. hole for the hinge pin. Set the lid in place on the box, and mark the centerpoint of the hole on the lid. Then drill through the lid and down into the wall of the box. Drill this 1⅞-in.-deep hole on the drill press, to ensure that the hole will be perfectly straight.

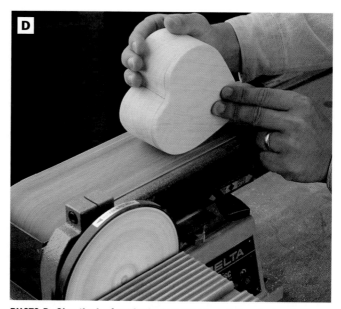

PHOTO D: Glue the kerf cut in the box closed, and glue the box bottom in place. Then smooth the edges of the box bottom where it meets the box sides with a stationary or orbital sander.

FINISHING TOUCHES

10 Apply the finish of your choice to all surfaces of the box and lid. We brushed on several coats of clear, satin polyurethane varnish, to show off the rich wood grain of the maple.

11 Install the hinge pin and lid: Enlarge the hinge pin hole in the lid slightly, so the lid swivels easily on the pin. Insert the pin through the lid hole, and apply glue into the hole in the box (**See Photo E**). Use the glue sparingly to minimize glue squeeze-out. Slip the hinge pin into its hole in the box.

PHOTO E: Drill a hole through the box lid and down into the box wall, using a drill press to bore the hole accurately. Drop a few dabs of glue into the hole in the box, and install the hinge pin. Be sure to keep the hole in the lid free of glue so the lid will swivel on the hinge pin.

Every young doll lover should have a cradle to rock toy babies to sleep. Here's a classic design that's a snap to build. It's proportions will fit most popular doll sizes. The cradle features dowels between the rockers on each side, so little ones can use their feet to rock the cradle. The cloverleaf-style cutouts add a touch of good luck for make-believe moms and dads.

Doll Cradle

Vital Statistics: Doll Cradle

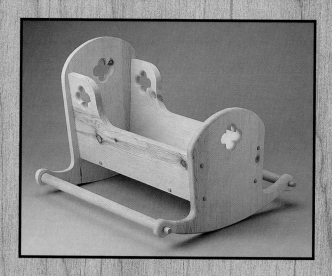

TYPE: Doll cradle

OVERALL SIZE: 18W by 19½L by 14¾H

MATERIAL: Pine

JOINERY: Glued, screwed and plugged butt joints

CONSTRUCTION DETAILS:

· Cloverleaf cutouts are created on the drill press
· Outside edges of headboard and footboard as well as cutouts are routed with ¼-in. roundover bit
· Ends of dowels are tenoned on the table saw to fit into round holes in the rocker ends
· Screws are counterbored and covered with button plugs

FINISH: Non-toxic clear varnish or paint

Building time

 PREPARING STOCK
1 hour

 LAYOUT
2 hours

 CUTTING PARTS
3-4 hours

 ASSEMBLY
2-3 hours

 FINISHING
1 hour

TOTAL: 9-11 hours

Tools you'll use

· Table saw
· Band saw
· Drill/driver
· Clamps
· Router with ¼-in. roundover bit
· Drill press
· Drum sander or drill press drum sanding kit
· 1-in. Forstner bit

Shopping list

☐ (1) ¾ × 10 in. × 10 ft. knotty pine

☐ (1) 1-in.-dia. × 4 ft. dowel

☐ #8 × 1½-in. flathead wood screws

☐ ⅜-in.-dia. wood buttons

☐ Wood glue

☐ Finishing materials

BUILD THE HEADBOARD & FOOTBOARD

1 You'll need 18-in.-wide stock for the headboard and footboard. To make blanks for these parts, first joint flat one long edge of your 1 × 10 pine stock. Crosscut two 14¾-in. lengths for the headboard and two 11-in. pieces for the footboard. Edge-glue and clamp the pairs of boards to form 18½-in.-wide blanks. After the glue dries, sand the blanks smooth.

2 Cut out the headboard and footboard: Transfer the *Headboard* and *Footboard* patterns on page 147 to your blanks. Cut the headboard and footboard to shape with a band saw or jig saw.

3 Smooth the edges: Clamp the headboard and footboard together so the edges of the rockers are flush, and gang-sand the rockers on a drum sander (**See Photo A**). This way, the rocker profiles will match. Remove the clamps and sand the rest of the edges. Then, rout around one edge of the headboard and one edge of the footboard with a ¼-in. roundover bit.

4 Drill holes in the rockers for the rails. Stack the headboard and footboard again so the edges of the rockers are flush, and mark the rail hole locations on the ends of the rockers. Bore ½-in.-dia. holes through both rockers at once on the drill press.

MAKE THE SIDES & BOTTOM

5 Cut out the sides and bottom: Rip and crosscut the side and bottom panels to size on the table saw. Then tilt the blade 5° and bevel-cut one long edge of the side panels. Cut the same 5° bevel along both long edges of the bottom. Be careful when bevel-cutting the bottom—the beveled edges need to mirror one another so the sides will cant away from the bottom when the doll cradle is assembled (See the exploded view drawing on page 146).

PHOTO A: After the headboard and footboard have been band-sawn to shape, clamp the pieces together so the rockers are flush. Smooth the rocker profiles on the drum sander until they'll match. Then unclamp the parts and smooth the rest of the cut edges.

Backer board

PHOTO B: Bore four holes to create the cloverleaf cutout pattern in the sides, headboard and footboard. Avoid tearout by clamping a scrap backer board to the drill press table.

6 Cut the top curved profiles in the sides: Transfer the *Sides* grid drawing on page 147 to one of the side panels. Since these profiles match on both side panels, stack the sides together and cut the curves into both workpieces at once on the band saw with the gridded piece on top. Sand the cut edges smooth.

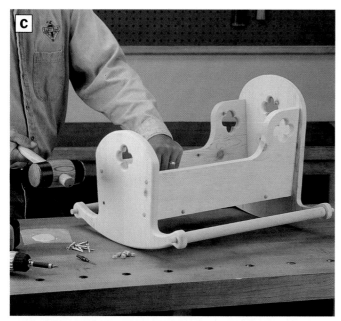

PHOTO C: Assemble the cradle parts with glue and flathead wood screws. Drill counterbored pilot holes to recess the screw heads. Then cover these screw heads with button-style wood plugs. Tap the plugs into their counterbores until they seat fully.

DRILL THE CUTOUTS

7 Drill cutouts in the headboard, footboard and sides: Mark the location of the cutouts on these parts. Then use the *Cutout Hole Drilling Pattern, page 147*, to find the centerpoints for drilling the four holes that make up each cutout. Bore holes for the cutouts through the cradle parts with a 1-in.-dia. Forstner or spade bit on the drill press **(See Photo B)**.

8 Ease the edges of the cutouts: Rout around both edges of each cutout on the headboard, footboard and sides with a ¼-in. piloted roundover bit. Sand these edges to remove any saw marks and router burns.

MAKE THE RAILS

9 Cut tenons on the ends of the rails. Crosscut the dowel rails to length first, then cut 1¼-in.-long, ½-in.-dia. round tenons on both ends of each rail (See *Cutting Round Tenons, right*). Smooth the tenons with a file and sandpaper, and check their fit in the holes in the rockers. The rails should swivel easily.

ASSEMBLE THE PARTS

10 Sand all the doll cradle parts with 220-grit sandpaper. Then dry-fit the pieces together to check their fit, and adjust as necessary.

11 Glue and screw the cradle together. Refer to the drawings on page 147 to mark pilot holes for attaching the headboard and footboard to the sides, as well

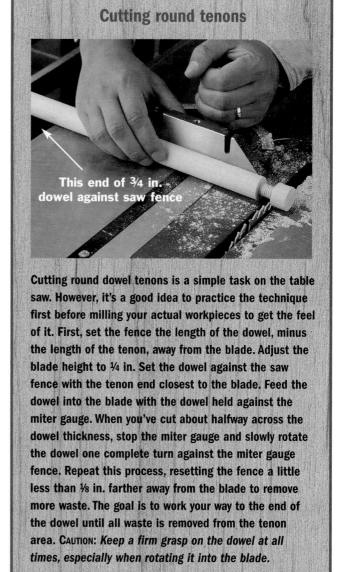

Cutting round tenons

This end of ¾ in. dowel against saw fence

Cutting round dowel tenons is a simple task on the table saw. However, it's a good idea to practice the technique first before milling your actual workpieces to get the feel of it. First, set the fence the length of the dowel, minus the length of the tenon, away from the blade. Adjust the blade height to ¼ in. Set the dowel against the saw fence with the tenon end closest to the blade. Feed the dowel into the blade with the dowel held against the miter gauge. When you've cut about halfway across the dowel thickness, stop the miter gauge and slowly rotate the dowel one complete turn against the miter gauge fence. Repeat this process, resetting the fence a little less than ⅛ in. farther away from the blade to remove more waste. The goal is to work your way to the end of the dowel until all waste is removed from the tenon area. CAUTION: *Keep a firm grasp on the dowel at all times, especially when rotating it into the blade.*

as attach the sides to the bottom. Join the sides to the bottom first with glue and 1½-in. flathead wood screws driven into counterbored pilot holes. Be sure the sides overlap the edges of the bottom piece. The sides should flare outward. Then set this assembly between the headboard and footboard and slip the rails into their holes in the rockers. Fasten these parts with counterbored wood screws and glue.

FINISHING TOUCHES

12 For a decorative touch, cover all exposed screwheads with ⅜-in. button-style wood plugs, secured with glue **(See Photo C)**.

13 Topcoat the cradle with a clear child-safe finish. We used three coats of satin polyurethane.

Tambour Breadbox

Atraditional gift that was beginning to lose favor, the breadbox has enjoyed a huge revival recently thanks to the incredible popularity of bread machines. Whether your bread comes from a machine or the corner bakery, you'll have ample storage for all your loaves in this classic breadbox. Our design features an attractive, easy-to-build tambour door and a storage drawer on top for bread knives.

Vital Statistics: Tambour Breadbox

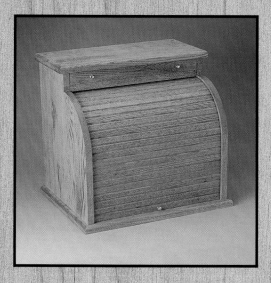

TYPE: Breadbox

OVERALL SIZE: 14½D by 18W by 16½H

MATERIAL: Red oak

JOINERY: Dadoes, rabbets and butt joints

CONSTRUCTION DETAILS:

- Tambour door staves glued and pressed to cotton fabric
- Door slides in grooves that are routed with a plywood template and ⅜-in. router guide bushing
- Drawer face is flush-fit to the drawer support and sides
- Drawer box assembled with interlocking rabbet-and-dado joints
- Drawer support fits into stopped dadoes in sides

FINISH: Wood stain and satin polyurethane varnish

Building time

PREPARING STOCK
2 hours

LAYOUT
4 hours

CUTTING PARTS
4-6 hours

ASSEMBLY
3 hours

FINISHING
2 hours

TOTAL: 15-17 hours

Tools you'll use

- Table saw
- Drill/driver
- Drill press
- Power miter saw (optional)
- Clamps
- Router table with ⅜-in. roundover bit, ⅜-in. guide bushing, ¼-, ½-, and ¾-in. straight bits
- Dado blade
- Carpenter's square
- J-roller
- ⅜-in. counterbore bit
- ⅜-in. plug cutter

Shopping list

- ☐ (2) ¾ × 8 in. × 8 ft. red oak
- ☐ (1) ¾ × 6 in. × 4 ft. red oak
- ☐ (1) ½ × 4 in. × 4 ft. red oak
- ☐ (1) ½ in. × 2 ft. × 2 ft. oak plywood
- ☐ (1) ¼ × 8 × 16 in. oak plywood
- ☐ #8 × 1½-in. flathead wood screws
- ☐ (1) 2 × 2 ft. heavy cotton fabric
- ☐ (3) ½-in.-dia. brass knobs
- ☐ Wood glue
- ☐ Finishing materials

BUILD THE SIDES

1 Make blanks for the sides: Crosscut one of the 1 × 8 oak boards into four 15-in. lengths, and flatten the edges on a jointer. Edge-glue and clamp the boards in pairs to form two blanks for the sides. Then rip the blanks to a final width of 14 in.

2 Cut the sides to shape: Use the *Detail: Sides* drawing, page 153, to lay out the shape of the sides on one of the two blanks. Trace this shape onto the second blank and cut to shape. Sand all the cut edges.

3 Rout grooves in the sides for the back and drawer support: Cut both grooves with straight bits in the router table. The ¼-in.-deep groove for the back panel is inset ¼ in. from the back edge of the sides and runs top to bottom. Mill this groove first with a ½-in. straight bit. The ¼-in.-deep shelf support dadoes are located 1⅜ in. in from the top end of the sides. They stop ½ in. from the front edge of the sides and intersect the groove for the back. Set up stopblocks on your router table to limit the length of these shelf support dadoes, then rout them into both side panels with a ¾-in. straight bit. Square up the front end of the shelf support dadoes with a sharp chisel.

4 Mill the tracks for the tambour door in the sides. To make these cuts accurately, build the *Tambour Groove Router Template* shown on page 153 from ¾-in. scrap, and sand it smooth. Mark the jig where the tambour track needs to stop. Install a ⅜-in.-dia. bushing and ¼-in. straight bit in your router. Align the flat edge of the jig with the bottom of the side panel, and so the router bit will cut the track groove ¼ in. in from the front curved edge of the side. Clamp the jig in place. Plow the track in two passes of increasing depth to a final depth of ¼ in. **(See Photo A)**. Be sure to stop the track groove cuts as indicated on your jig. Set up and clamp the jig on the other side panel, and rout a matching track.

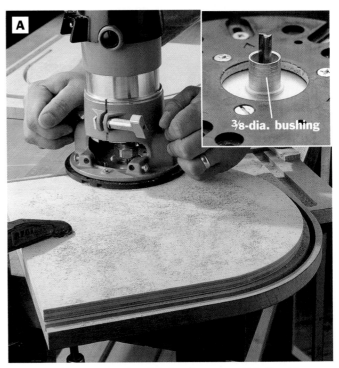

PHOTO A: After the router template has been secured to the sides, begin milling the tracks for the tambour door. Install a ⅜-in. bushing and ¼-in. straight bit on your router (See inset photo) to make these cuts. Be sure to mark the template so you know where the tracks should end. Rout the tracks in two passes.

⅜-dia. bushing

PHOTO B: Glue and install the back and drawer support into their grooves in the sides. Clamp up this assembly to hold the joints closed until the glue dries.

PHOTO C: Attach the top and bottom to the carcase so they overhang the sides evenly. The bottom gets attached only with countersunk screws for now—it will need to be removed to install the tambour door. The top is attached with glue as well as countersunk screws. Cover the screw heads with ⅜-in. oak plugs, then trim and sand the plugs flush.

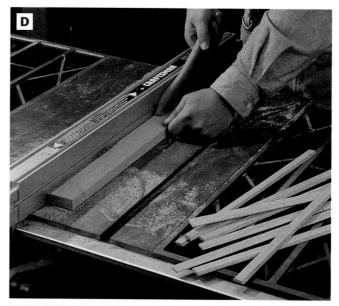

PHOTO D: After chamfering both long edges of a ¾-in.-thick oak blank, set your table saw fence ³⁄₁₆ in. from the blade and rip-cut the chamfered staves from the blank. Use a pushstick when feeding the blank through the blade to keep your fingers clear. Repeat this process until you've cut 23 staves.

MAKE THE REMAINING CARCASE PARTS

❺ Build the top and bottom: Make a blank for the bottom by edge-gluing two lengths of 1 × 8 stock together, and form another blank for the top from edge-glued 1 × 6. Rip the top and bottom to final width, and sand the edges and ends smooth. Ease the ends and one long edge around one face of both parts with a ⅜-in. roundover bit in the router table.

❻ Rip and crosscut the plywood back panel to size, according to the *Cutting List* dimensions, page 152.

❼ Prepare the drawer support. First, rip and crosscut the drawer support to size, then trim away the front corners of the drawer support with a band saw so it will sit flush with the front of the sides and fit around and into the stopped grooves (See *Detail: Drawer Support Notched Corners,* page 153).

ASSEMBLE THE CARCASE

❽ Glue and fasten the carcase parts together. First, dry-assemble the back and drawer support in the sides to test the fit. Then glue these parts into their grooves, clamp up the assembly and check for square (**See Photo B**). When the glue dries, attach the top to the sides. Be sure the bullnosed edge of the top faces up and forward and the flat edge is flush with the back of the sides. The top should overhang the sides evenly. Mark the top for four screws, then glue and fasten it in place with counterbored, 1½-in. wood

screws. Set the carcase on the bottom panel, with the bullnosed edge facing up and forward. Attach the bottom to the sides temporarily with countersunk wood screws; you'll need to remove it to install the door.

❾ Cover the counterbored screw heads in the top with ⅜-in.-dia. oak plugs (**See Photo C**). Then trim and sand the plugs flush.

BUILD THE TAMBOUR DOOR

The tambour door consists of 23 staves butted edge to edge and glued to a sheet of cotton material, which provides a rugged but flexible backing for the door to bend. To mill the thin staves efficiently and safely, you'll chamfer the top and bottom edges of an oak blank and rip-cut one stave at a time from the blank, chamfering again before ripping the next stave. Or you could buy premilled tambour instead of making it (See *Prefabricated Tambour,* next page).

❿ Make the staves. Begin by chucking a 45° piloted chamfering bit in your router table and set the bit height to ³⁄₃₂ in. Crosscut a ¾-in.-thick blank of oak stock to 15¹⁵⁄₁₆ in. long. Set the fence on your table saw ³⁄₁₆ in. from the blade. Mill each stave by chamfering both the top and bottom edges of the blank, then slicing the chamfered edges off on the table saw (**See Photo D**). Plane away any saw marks left on the cut edges of the blank, and repeat the chamfering and ripping process until you've made 23 staves.

PHOTO E: Cradle the staves in the crook of a carpenter's square clamped to a sheet of hardboard. Hold the staves together with strips of wide masking tape to prepare for glue-up.

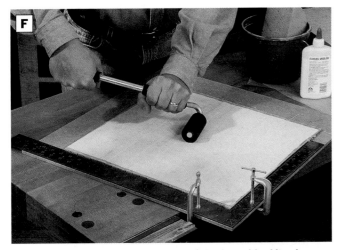

PHOTO F: Attach cloth to the back side of the door with white glue, wetting the cloth slightly with a sponge to draw the glue into the cloth. Then use a J-roller to smooth out any wrinkles or bubbles. Press the cloth flat by setting heavy objects such as bricks or a bucket of water on top of the staves with a layer of wax paper beneath.

PHOTO G: Trim the ends of the cloth back about ⅜ in. from the ends of the staves. This way, the bare ends of the staves will slide more easily in their tracks.

⑪ Assemble the staves: Butt the staves tightly together, chamfered-face up, against the inside of a carpenter's square clamped to a piece of hardboard. The carpenter's square will help align the ends of the staves. Once the staves are aligned, hold the outermost stave in place with scrap blocks and spring clamps. Temporarily join the staves with three strips of wide masking tape (See Photo E).

⑫ Cut a piece of cotton fabric (about the weight of denim) large enough to cover the width of all the staves and about ¼ in. short of the ends. Wash and dry the cloth before you cut it to size to minimize shrinkage later.

⑬ Glue the staves to the cloth. Flip the stave assembly over in the carpenter's square jig so the chamfered edges face down, and spread a thin, even coating of white glue over all of the stave backs. Lay the cloth on the staves and dampen the back with a wet sponge. Press the cloth into the glue and smooth any wrinkles with a J-roller (See Photo F). Cover the cloth with wax paper. Place weights (bricks, cement pavers, a bucket of water) on the wax paper and let the glue dry overnight.

⑭ Fit the door in the door tracks. Trim excess cloth from the ends of the staves with a straightedge and a utility knife (See Photo G). Remove enough cloth so about ⅜ in. of ends of the staves are bare. Unscrew

Prefabricated tambour

If you'd rather not build tambour, you can purchase it in numerous species and in a huge variety of stave dimensions and designs from woodworking supply catalogs. The most common form is a canvas-backed tambour sheet, but it is also sold as a series of staves with a sheet of paper glued to the front face. After attaching the staves to a cloth backing, you sand the paper off to expose the staves. Some manufacturers even offer tambour that requires no backing: the edges of the individual staves are profiled so that they interlock with each other, in effect forming a series of long hinges. There are even tambour sheets with the staves held together by strings, much in the way that window blinds are constructed. Do not mill any parts for your project until you have the tambour in hand.

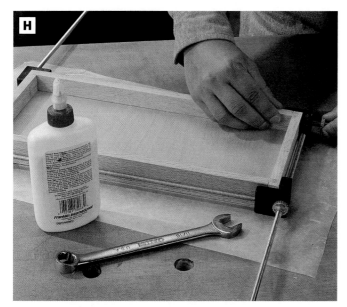

PHOTO H: A frame clamp is a convenient way to glue up the drawer, because it keeps the assembly square. Glue the corner joints only. Leave the bottom floating in its dadoes to allow for wood movement.

PHOTO I: After the finish has been applied, install two brass pulls on the drawer and one to the bottom door stave. You'll need to buy 1¼-in.-long machine screws for the drawer knobs and a ⅜-in.-long machine screw for the knob on the tambour door.

the bottom from the breadbox carcase and slide the door into its grooves. Sand the bare ends of the staves as needed until the door slides easily along the full tracks but still holds position at any point along the tracks. Then remove the door for finishing.

MAKE THE DRAWER

15 Machine the drawer parts: Rip and crosscut the drawer face, front, back and sides from ½-in.-thick oak stock. Plow a ¼-in.-wide, ¼-in.-deep groove across the width of the inside face of the drawer sides, ¼-in. in from each end (See *Detail: Drawer Corner Joints,* page 153). Make these cuts on the table saw with a dado blade or on the router table with a ¼-in. straight bit. Using the same cutter, mill ¼-in.-deep dadoes in the drawer sides, front and back, ⅛ in. from the bottom edge and along its length for the drawer bottom. Finally, cut ¼ × ¼-in. rabbets into the ends of the outside face (the face opposite the drawer bottom dadoes) of the drawer front and back. These rabbets form tongues that fit into the short dadoes in the drawer sides.

16 Assemble the drawer: Dry-fit the sides to the front and back with the drawer bottom in its grooves, and make any necessary adjustments. The dadoes and rabbets form strong interlocking joints at the drawer corners. Disassemble the drawer, glue up the corner joints, slip the drawer bottom into its grooves (without glue) and assemble the drawer box. Use a frame clamp or other small bar clamps to hold the joints closed until the glue dries **(See Photo H)**.

17 Install the drawer face: Attach the drawer face to the drawer front with glue. Hold the drawer face in position with spring clamps. Drill pilot holes through the drawer face and drawer front, and screw on the two drawer knobs 2½ in. from each end of the drawer. You'll need 1¼-in.-long machine screws for securing these knobs.

FINISHING TOUCHES

18 Sand and finish the breadbox: Remove the drawer and knobs, and sand the surfaces of all of the breadbox parts with 220-grit sandpaper. Remove any residual dust with a tack cloth. Apply the stain of your choice (or one to match your existing cabinetry). Finish all surfaces (inside and out) with three coats of clear polyurethane varnish. NOTE: *There's no need to varnish the tambour cloth.*

19 Slide the door into its tracks, and screw the breadbox bottom back on the carcase.

20 Install the tambour door knob: Drill a centered pilot hole through the bottom stave. You'll need a ⅜-in.-long machine screw to fasten the knob on the stave **(See Photo I)**.

Index

Index of Projects